QlikView Unlocked

Unlock more than 50 amazing tips and tricks to enhance your QlikView skills

Roger Stone

Andrew Dove

BIRMINGHAM - MUMBAI

QlikView Unlocked

Copyright © 2015 Packt Publishing

All rights reserved. No part of this book may be reproduced, stored in a retrieval system, or transmitted in any form or by any means, without the prior written permission of the publisher, except in the case of brief quotations embedded in critical articles or reviews.

Every effort has been made in the preparation of this book to ensure the accuracy of the information presented. However, the information contained in this book is sold without warranty, either express or implied. Neither the authors, nor Packt Publishing, and its dealers and distributors will be held liable for any damages caused or alleged to be caused directly or indirectly by this book.

Packt Publishing has endeavored to provide trademark information about all of the companies and products mentioned in this book by the appropriate use of capitals. However, Packt Publishing cannot guarantee the accuracy of this information.

First published: November 2015

Production reference: 1051115

Published by Packt Publishing Ltd.
Livery Place
35 Livery Street
Birmingham B3 2PB, UK.

ISBN 978-1-78528-512-7

www.packtpub.com

Credits

Authors
Roger Stone
Andrew Dove

Reviewers
Christopher Murrell
Xavier Segado Recio
David Stone

Acquisition Editor
Subho Gupta

Content Development Editor
Dharmesh Parmar

Technical Editor
Siddhesh Ghadi

Copy Editor
Shruti Iyer

Project Coordinator
Paushali Desai

Proofreader
Safis Editing

Indexer
Mariammal Chettiyar

Graphics
Disha Haria

Production Coordinator
Conidon Miranda

Cover Work
Conidon Miranda

About the Authors

Roger Stone is a freelance QlikView consultant based in Oxfordshire, UK. He entered the computer industry in 1977 and has worked with a huge variety of programming languages and tools all over the world. Finally discovering QlikView in late 2009, he has worked on numerous successful QlikView implementations in a wide range of industries, from insurance to healthcare.

In 2010, Roger founded One QV Ltd with coauthor Andrew Dove, and together they developed 1HR, a QlikView-based human resources application aimed at the National Health Service in the UK. 1HR has since been deployed to more than 25 NHS Trusts.

He currently holds QlikView Designer, Developer, and Systems Administrator Certifications for QlikView 11. Roger enjoys travel, Belgian beer, and military history, all of which are combined in his frequent trips to Belgium.

Andrew Dove is a freelance QlikView consultant based in Darlington, UK. He has more than 35 years of experience in various IT development roles and developed a highly successful payroll system in the 1980s and 90s.

Andrew began his QlikView journey in 2010 and joined coauthor Roger Stone to found One QV Ltd. He has since worked on several large QlikView projects in healthcare, manufacturing, pharmaceuticals, and financial services.

Andrew holds QlikView Designer, Developer, and Systems Administrator Certifications for QlikView 11. He enjoys travel, French wine, and cheese, all of which feature in his frequent trips to France.

About the Reviewers

Christopher Murrell is a QlikView consultant who started working with business intelligence tools during a year in industry placement while at university. He has worked in a variety of roles, including network administration, web development, C# programming, and data analytics, before starting with QlikView in 2010. Since then, Christopher has worked in a wide range of industries, including insurance and medical research with the National Health Service in the UK, and Australian Health Service in Melbourne, Australia.

Xavier Segado Recio is a hybrid senior data/process/business analyst and applications trainer with over 30 years of experience in the IT industry. His experience spans numerous applications, products, tools, and industries, including retail, accounting, IT methodologies, distribution, pharmaceuticals, healthcare, and treasury services.

Xavier currently works as a BI specialist with a leading UK property group, where he uses QlikView as a tool to change the way information is managed and used.

David Stone first started using QlikView in 2010, testing dashboards built by One QV Ltd. He worked on several small projects for the company while still at university, honing his design and development skills, and he eventually joined a UK-based Qlik partner after graduating in 2013. After 18 months there and having covered all aspects of QlikView development in a leading investment bank, he moved to his current role. He is now busy architecting and developing new QlikView solutions for one of Europe's largest online casino and sports betting companies. David lives in London and enjoys traveling and sampling new beers.

www.PacktPub.com

Support files, eBooks, discount offers, and more

For support files and downloads related to your book, please visit www.PacktPub.com.

Did you know that Packt offers eBook versions of every book published, with PDF and ePub files available? You can upgrade to the eBook version at www.PacktPub.com and as a print book customer, you are entitled to a discount on the eBook copy. Get in touch with us at service@packtpub.com for more details.

At www.PacktPub.com, you can also read a collection of free technical articles, sign up for a range of free newsletters and receive exclusive discounts and offers on Packt books and eBooks.

https://www2.packtpub.com/books/subscription/packtlib

Do you need instant solutions to your IT questions? PacktLib is Packt's online digital book library. Here, you can search, access, and read Packt's entire library of books.

Why subscribe?

- Fully searchable across every book published by Packt
- Copy and paste, print, and bookmark content
- On demand and accessible via a web browser

Free access for Packt account holders

If you have an account with Packt at www.PacktPub.com, you can use this to access PacktLib today and view 9 entirely free books. Simply use your login credentials for immediate access.

Instant updates on new Packt books

Get notified! Find out when new books are published by following @PacktEnterprise on Twitter or the *Packt Enterprise* Facebook page.

Table of Contents

Preface	**vii**
Chapter 1: Behind Every Successful Project Is a Plan	**1**
Why infrastructure is important	**1**
Background	1
How to do it	2
Environments and architecture	**5**
Background	5
How to do it	6
Building a reusable, maintainable environment	**9**
Background	9
How to do it	10
QlikView projects need discipline too!	**12**
Background	13
How to do it	13
Can you deliver?	**14**
Background	14
How to do it	15
Summary	**16**
Chapter 2: Building the Correct Environment	**17**
Creating and enforcing site standards	**17**
Background	17
How to do it	18
Designing a site-style template	**22**
Background	22
How to do it	22
Making document names meaningful	**26**
Background	26
How to do it	27

Separation of responsibilities, change management, and thinking about security — 28
Background — 28
How to do it — 29
Understanding the differences in environments — 31
Background — 31
How to do it — 31
With or without Publisher? — 32
Summary — 34

Chapter 3: Are You Sitting Comfortably? Be More Productive — 35
A bit more about license types — 35
Background — 35
How to do it — 36
Make yourself comfortable and productive — 38
Background — 39
How to do it — 39
Most recently used files — 40
Selection appearance — 40
Search settings — 40
Max values in current selections — 41
Never lose your work — 41
Background — 41
How to do it — 42
Some useful global settings — 43
Background — 43
How to do it — 43
Default Styling Mode — 44
Always Use Logfiles for New Documents — 46
Always Show Design Menu Items — 46
Some best practices for developers — 47
Background — 47
How to do it — 48
Hidden features – Easter eggs — 48
Background — 49
How to do it — 49
A few do's and don'ts — 51
Background — 51
How to do it — 51
Summary — 52

Chapter 4: It's All About Understanding the Data — 53
Understanding the data you're working with — 53
Background — 54
How to do it — 54
Even a few list and table boxes tell you and the user a lot — 55
Background — 55
How to do it — 56
Exciting users with a prototype, then throwing it away — 60
Background — 60
How to do it — 60
Dirty data and what to do about it — 61
Background — 61
How to do it — 62
- Incorrect or erroneous data — 62
- Inconsistent data — 63
- Duplication — 65
Is this the right place for this data? — 65
Background — 65
How to do it — 66
Building a structure of QVD layers — 67
Background — 67
How to do it — 67
Incremental loads and performance — 71
Background — 71
How to do it — 71
- Performance — 75
Summary — 76

Chapter 5: The Right Data Model Pays Dividends — 77
Synthetic keys and why they're sometimes bad news — 77
Background — 77
How to do it — 78
Link tables — 80
Background — 80
How to do it — 80
Avoiding loops in the data model — 83
Background — 83
How to do it — 83

Simplify, simplify, simplify – never have subtables that you don't need	**85**
Background	85
How to do it	85
Data islands, single calendars, and set analysis	**89**
Background	89
How to do it	90
Avoiding problems with JOIN	**92**
Background	92
How to do it	92
Summary	**96**
Chapter 6: Make It Easy on Yourself – Some QlikView Tips and Tricks	**97**
A few coding tips	**97**
Keep the coding style constant	98
Use MUST_INCLUDE rather than INCLUDE	98
Put version numbers in your code	98
Do stringing in the script, not in screen objects	98
Surprising data sources	**99**
Include files	**101**
Change logs	**102**
Calculations and flags in the script	**103**
Previous() and Peek() functions	**108**
Preceding load on preceding load	**109**
Finding min and max	**110**
Autonumber	**112**
Reading from a spreadsheet	**112**
Summary	**113**
Chapter 7: Improving Chart Performance and Usability	**115**
Don't forget screen performance	**115**
Cached expressions	**116**
Multiple selection criteria	**117**
Copying expressions	**120**
Reusing chart expressions	**121**
Hidden graphics	**122**
Making charts more readable	**122**
Helping the user – Help Text	124
Resizing objects	**127**

Stopping objects from being moved	**128**
Defaulting the scroll bar to the right of a chart	**131**
Summary	**133**
Chapter 8: To Deployment and Beyond	**135**
Security and Section Access	**135**
Explanation	135
Background	136
How to do it	136
Physical Network Access	136
Document CALs	136
With Publisher	136
Section Access	138
Hiding fields	143
Passing additional parameters	144
Section Access with Data Reduction and QlikView Publisher	146
Why server jobs fail	**147**
Connection failures	147
Excel spreadsheets	147
Drive letters	148
QlikView engines	148
Antivirus software	149
QVD	149
Deploying from development to UAT and on to production	**149**
Explanation	149
Background	150
How to do it	150
The golden source	**150**
Explanation	151
Background	151
How to do it	151
Why Publisher isn't always a good thing	**152**
Explanation	152
Background	152
How to do it	152
Your two best friends	**153**
Explanation	153
Background	153
How to do it	153

It will never be perfect but it will be close	**156**
Explanation	156
Background	156
How to do it	156
Summary	**157**
Appendix: Hidden Image List	**159**
Index	**169**

Preface

Welcome to *QlikView Unlocked*. We hope that you find this book a useful guide when planning, executing, or maintaining a QlikView deployment. This book isn't intended to be a "mastering" guide, nor is it intended to teach you the basics of QlikView. We're assuming that you have been using QlikView for a while and are looking to expand your knowledge. We will highlight some important or interesting things for you to consider along with some guidance on best practices. You don't have to read the book from cover to cover; just dip into the chapters when you're interested in a particular topic. Things get more technical further into the book. *Chapter 5*, *The Right Data Model Pays Dividends* and beyond will be of most interest to developers, but we think there's something for everyone in every chapter.

The QlikView Unlocked project

In order to put some of the explanations into context, we based the book loosely around a project, but this is only for the sake of consistency in the examples. We will not give you a step-by-step guide to learning QlikView, which is what you might find in some *teach yourself* books, instead we will focus on insights that will give you an edge and show you things that you probably didn't realize could be done with QlikView. For this, we created a project at Borchester Models, a fictitious chain of model shops. Their business is the sale of unusual, short-run plastic aircraft kits. The chain has three shops in different towns in Borsetshire, the Borchester shop being the head office.

They have a website that sells a few models online, but most sales are through their point of sale system that runs in all three shops. We'll use some of the situations that might be encountered in this simple QlikView implementation for the examples in this book.

QlikView is huge

If you're reading this book, chances are that you belong to the growing army of QlikView professionals. So, when we say QlikView is huge, not only do we mean that it's big news, but also that it's a big product. On the surface, QlikView is just another programming tool. In reality, it's a complete, powerful, and very sophisticated environment. It sometimes seems that there's just no end to the things you can do with QlikView. While the focus is very much on being a powerful business intelligence tool, we have seen QlikView documents that draw a rotating Christmas tree complete with lights, a media player, and an analog clock (QlokView—brilliant!). We hope you enjoy using QlikView as much as we do and maintain the momentum by following up on some of the ideas in this book. Stay keen and keep your users or customers engaged by offering them new and interesting insights that you will find in all the following sources.

Qlik Community

QlikView people are, on the whole, a very helpful lot. Sometimes, we all come across a problem that we don't know how to solve or are maybe just curious as to how some piece of functionality works. We all know that no manual covers every situation, but fortunately, there are people out there who have seen most. You will find that many of them hang out on Qlik Community (`https://community.qlik.com/welcome`), and they know a heck of a lot about QlikView. Always try searching for an answer first, but when you're stuck, ask a question. Chances are someone will have the answer. Don't forget to mark the response as "Helpful" or "Answered"—and say thanks too. These people do it because, well, they're helpful and love messing around with QlikView.

LinkedIn

If you haven't joined any of the LinkedIn QlikView groups, we encourage you to do so. Qlik Community is the best place for technical questions and answers, but LinkedIn has more general discussions about Qlik products and a number of groups dedicated to jobs. If you're looking for your next QlikView job or contract, QlikView Gigs is a good place to start. Members include recruiters and hiring managers as well as QlikView professionals.

QlikView blogs

Many of the experts on Qlik Community also have their own blogs, and these can be a great place to pick up new tips and tricks.

If you want to see *a lot* of blogs, try `www.askqv.com/blogs/`; at the time of writing this, it lists 37 QlikView blogs of varying quality and frequency of postings.

Books about QlikView

The last couple of years have seen a number of books about QlikView appear on bookshelves, many of these published by Packt Publishing. They're all very useful to anyone serious about getting the best out of QlikView.

Service releases

Some of the things to keep an eye out for are the regular **service releases** (**SRs**) of QlikView. Each SR has a number of bug fixes and often some minor improvements to functionality. At the time we started writing this book (March 2015), QlikView was at version 11.2 SR10. As we draw to the end of writing (July 2015), version 11.2 SR12 is out. Qlik are set to release QlikView 12 later in 2015, and this will be the first major release in about four years. We encourage you to look out for it as there will be some exciting new features.

Qlik events

Every year, usually around October, Qlik has a world tour, showcasing new features and customer applications. If you only get out of the office once a year, try to get along to one of these events. You'll see some great innovations and hear lots of interesting QlikView stories.

From time to time, Qlik runs smaller local events, often in conjunction with a partner. These normally focus on a specific business area and are usually by invitation only. It's worth going along if the topic is relevant to your business.

If you're working for a Qlik Partner, there's another *must see* event, and this is Qonnections. Up to 2015, this partner-only event was held each April usually in the USA. Along with presentations about product direction and new features in QlikView and Qlik Sense, there are numerous workshops on a wide range of topics, from sales and marketing to very technical sessions. If you get the chance to go along sometime, take it. In 2016, we understand that it will be open to partners, customers, and prospects, so it will be a massive event. They have beer too, and there's a lively social side; so, come prepared for several days of intense QlikView, lots of partying, and little sleep.

Local groups

If you really can't get enough of QlikView, we know of a few local groups that you can go along to. Here, you can swap stories with other Qlikkies, and there will usually be a presentation or two on specific QlikView or Qlik Sense topics. Try searching LinkedIn groups to see if there's a physical meeting in your area. If you're in or around London, UK, you might like to attend one of the meetings organized by Qlik Dev Group (www.qlikdevgroup.com).

What this book covers

Chapter 1, Behind Every Successful Project Is a Plan, covers the basics of a QlikView environment, how to organize a QlikView project, and how to ensure that the development has clear deliverables.

Chapter 2, Building the Correct Environment, sets standards for the project or site as a whole, understanding that getting the environment right is a vital foundation for everything else.

Chapter 3, Are you Sitting Comfortably? Be More Productive, discusses some useful settings for the desktop workbench that save lots of time and open up features, making development more productive.

Chapter 4, It's All About Understanding the Data, looks at data and how it relates to the task at hand as well as at prototyping, how to correctly structure the data environment for performance and ease of use, and how to tackle common data problems.

Chapter 5, The Right Data Model Pays Dividends, identifies and fixes issues in the data model that could cause poor performance or difficulties in presenting data to the user.

Chapter 6, Make It Easy on Yourself–Some QlikView Tips and Tricks, provides you with some great time-saving tips.

Chapter 7, Improving Chart Performance and Usability, helps you unlock the power of charting by understanding little-known features and nonstandard ways of presenting data.

Chapter 8, *To Deployment and Beyond*, talks about how to implement security, deploy and protect the source code, and how to investigate and solve problems on QlikView Server.

Appendix, *Hidden Image List*, provides over 450 built-in images that can be used in any QlikView document.

What you need for this book

For the examples in this book, you need to have QlikView Personal Edition, version 11.2 with a recent Service Release (preferably SR9 or later).

Who this book is for

QlikView Unlocked is intended for anyone with at least some experience in designing, developing, or supporting QlikView applications. This book is carefully constructed so that the subjects discussed become more advanced in later chapters. Whether new to QlikView or a seasoned developer, there is something for everyone in this book.

Conventions

In this book, you will find a number of text styles that distinguish between different kinds of information. Here are some examples of these styles and an explanation of their meaning.

Code words in text, database table names, folder names, filenames, file extensions, pathnames, dummy URLs, user input, and Twitter handles are shown as follows: "This can be stored in the `9. Documentation` subfolder."

A block of code is set as follows:

```
Stock:
LOAD [Shop No],
     [Product Code],
     [On Hand]
FROM
[QlikView Unlocked Data.xlsx]
(ooxml, embedded labels, table is Stock);
```

When we wish to draw your attention to a particular part of a code block, the relevant lines or items are set in bold:

```
Stock:
LOAD [Shop No],
     [Product Code],
     [On Hand]
FROM
[QlikView Unlocked Data.xlsx]
(ooxml, embedded labels, table is Stock);
```

New terms and **important words** are shown in bold. Words that you see on the screen, for example, in menus or dialog boxes, appear in the text like this: "Clicking the **Next** button moves you to the next screen."

> Warnings or important notes appear in a box like this.

> Tips and tricks appear like this.

Reader feedback

Feedback from our readers is always welcome. Let us know what you think about this book—what you liked or disliked. Reader feedback is important for us as it helps us develop titles that you will really get the most out of.

To send us general feedback, simply e-mail feedback@packtpub.com, and mention the book's title in the subject of your message.

If there is a topic that you have expertise in and you are interested in either writing or contributing to a book, see our author guide at www.packtpub.com/authors.

Customer support

Now that you are the proud owner of a Packt book, we have a number of things to help you to get the most from your purchase.

Downloading the color images of this book

We also provide you with a PDF file that has color images of the screenshots/diagrams used in this book. The color images will help you better understand the changes in the output. You can download this file from https://www.packtpub.com/sites/default/files/downloads/5127EN_ColorImages.pdf.

Errata

Although we have taken every care to ensure the accuracy of our content, mistakes do happen. If you find a mistake in one of our books—maybe a mistake in the text or the code—we would be grateful if you could report this to us. By doing so, you can save other readers from frustration and help us improve subsequent versions of this book. If you find any errata, please report them by visiting http://www.packtpub.com/submit-errata, selecting your book, clicking on the **Errata Submission Form** link, and entering the details of your errata. Once your errata are verified, your submission will be accepted and the errata will be uploaded to our website or added to any list of existing errata under the Errata section of that title.

To view the previously submitted errata, go to https://www.packtpub.com/books/content/support and enter the name of the book in the search field. The required information will appear under the **Errata** section.

Piracy

Piracy of copyrighted material on the Internet is an ongoing problem across all media. At Packt, we take the protection of our copyright and licenses very seriously. If you come across any illegal copies of our works in any form on the Internet, please provide us with the location address or website name immediately so that we can pursue a remedy.

Please contact us at copyright@packtpub.com with a link to the suspected pirated material.

We appreciate your help in protecting our authors and our ability to bring you valuable content.

Questions

If you have a problem with any aspect of this book, you can contact us at questions@packtpub.com, and we will do our best to address the problem.

1
Behind Every Successful Project Is a Plan

In this chapter, we will cover the following key topics:

- Why infrastructure is important
- Environments and architecture
- Building a reusable, maintainable environment
- QlikView projects need discipline too!
- Can you deliver?

Why infrastructure is important

As QlikView deployments get bigger, the need to have suitable infrastructure becomes increasingly important.

Background

When embarking on a QlikView implementation, we don't always have the luxury of being able to design the whole environment and to choose the hardware, operating system, or machines at our disposal. Project history, budget constraints, and growth in the use of QlikView within the organization could all have an impact on the environment we have to work with. Small QlikView deployments will usually perform well on even a fairly modest hardware platform, but for large and growing deployments, care is needed to ensure optimal performance.

How to do it

QlikView is efficient and fast, but its performance can be compromised by the environment it operates in. Many organizations today have moved to virtualization, often with numerous virtual machines running on the same physical server. QlikView runs in a virtualized environment, but its performance can be adversely affected. While a virtualized development environment is fine, you should consider a physical machine for production.

The choice of hardware can be surprisingly important to QlikView. Fast processors and huge amounts of memory are not necessarily the answer to every performance issue. In fact, the speed at which data can move between memory and processor can be more important—which is obvious, really, considering that QlikView operates in memory. Not all chip sets have the bandwidth to maximize performance.

Performance isn't only about the server, of course. At the presentation level, the choice of browser is also important. This is something you'll have to test for yourself as each QlikView document behaves differently. Qlik supplies an IE plugin in the Server installation package, and this works well. However, if yours is a mixed browser environment or one in which tablets are used, it's worth considering whether to deploy the plugin at all. You could potentially have very different user experiences for the same QlikView document in plugin and nonplugin situations. The plugin takes some of the load off the server and tends to render pages better; so, in an IE-only environment, it is probably the best choice for user experience. The downside is that there's a maintenance implication when new releases of QlikView need to be implemented.

Here's a simple example of the differences in rendering, using rounded corners for a text object, and having shadows around a table object. We will create a text object that says **OK** and a basic table.

The following image depicts the settings for the text object:

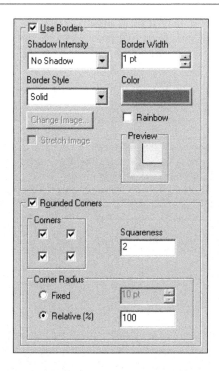

The following image depicts the settings for the table object:

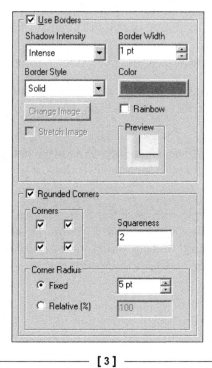

As rendered by the IE plugin, it will look like:

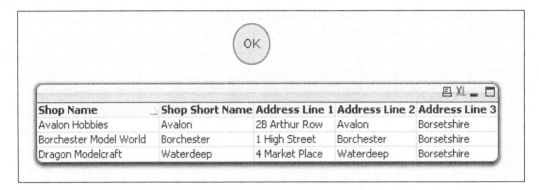

Here's how the object will look as rendered by IE without the plugin:

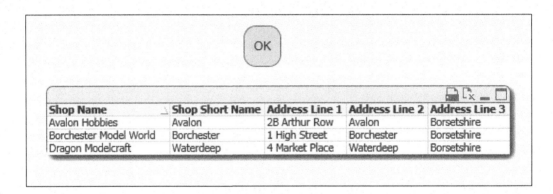

This simple example demonstrates that even the most basic elements of your environment can and will affect user experience before you even consider processors or memory!

Experimentation is a good thing; so, before choosing whether or not to use the IE plugin, do some experiments with layouts including, if possible, large calculations in the UI.

If you have the opportunity to influence the choice of hardware, consider referring to the whitelist published by Qlik Scalability Centre. This document is updated from time to time and is based on actual customer experiences. It covers processors, memory, architecture, BIOS, and Windows' settings.

Qlik or your partner can help you calculate how much memory you need, but you need to provide some basic pieces of information: a rough estimate of the number of rows, the width of these rows in terms of columns and the width of the columns themselves, the uniqueness of data (timestamps are more unique than dates, for example), and a reasonable estimate of the number of concurrent users. Despite everyone's best efforts, it is still very hard to come up with a precise answer to this question as there are simply too many variables. In fact, the only way to know reasonably accurately how much memory will be required is to create the solution first! This is a classic case of a chicken-and-egg situation, not helped by the fact that you'll almost certainly be creating multiple applications as time goes on.

There is more useful information about optimal server settings at `https://community.qlik.com/docs/DOC-2362`, covering topics such as hyperthreading, power management, and node interleaving. If you only read one document about settings for optimal performance, be it setting up a new implementation or running an existing one, make it this one.

Environments and architecture

The size of your QlikView deployment, budget, and future plans will directly influence the way the environment is built.

Background

In the simplest QlikView Server installation, you have a single machine (physical or virtual), where all development, user testing, and production takes place. There's nothing that wrong with this approach, and we've seen plenty of smaller installations where this is the case. A better solution, though, is to at least keep development and production separate. However, larger deployments and those requiring more control over access to QlikView documents tend towards multiple machines: one each for development, user testing, and production. If you use QlikView Publisher, you may wish to put this on its own server. Obviously, there is a cost implication as multiple Server licenses are required if QlikView is installed on more than one machine, and the Publisher license is an additional cost as it's not included in the QlikView Server license.

A further consideration in larger deployments or for mission-critical systems is whether to go for multiple production machines, employing load balancing and clustering.

How to do it

As with all things, the way the environment is built depends on what you need to deliver and to whom. Let's consider a few example scenarios. Hopefully, one of these will help guide you toward your goal. We'll assume, in all cases, that you could have the option of carrying out all development on PCs so that you only need effectively to design test and production environments. Bear in mind that the development PCs, unless running standalone desktop licenses, need access to a server at least every 30 days to renew their licenses, which could be a problem if you spend long periods off-site. There's a further "gotcha" here, too: if you use QlikView Test Server licenses, you cannot renew the PC license from them. It has to be done from the 'full' server license. Clearly, if developers are not supposed to have access to the production server, this has a security implication.

We would normally think of having three environments: **Development**, **Test** and **Production** (or **Live**). How these are implemented will depend on the number of machines at your disposal. Ideally you would have three or more, but of course there will be a cost implication because QlikView Server is licensed on a per machine basis. Therefore it is cheaper to implement on only one or two server machines but implementing on three or more will give a more robust and clearly-defined environment. Let's consider the options, based on one, two, three or more machines:

- **Single machine**: This is a simple environment. Development, testing, and production all reside on the same machine. QlikView Publisher may also be on the same machine. Take care to ensure that users know whether they're looking at test or production. You can separate these using different mounted folders in QlikView Management Console.
- **Two machines**: The big question here is whether the test environment should be on the development machine or the production machine. For safety's sake, we would always keep the test environment on the development machine.

- **Three machines**: These are deployed as development, test, and production. This is a nice, easy solution that keeps everything tidy and offers the greatest safety and control in terms of code versions. It is tempting to think that the test server could be used as a fallback in the event of production server failure. We would avoid this as it would require quite a lot of work, so unless you can reimage the test server as a production server quickly and cleanly, this is probably not a good strategy.
- **Multiple machines**: Stepping into enterprise-level environments leads to a wide variety of options with opportunities for load balancing and clustering. In large deployments, development and test most likely stay on separate machines but production is spread across two or more machines. This allows for greater resilience in the event of the failure of a production server and gives the opportunity for horizontal scalability. As more users are added, the environment can be scaled out with more servers. It is possible to arrange a cluster in such a way that all documents can be served by any of the machines, giving great resilience. QlikView Publisher can also be clustered, providing similar resilience and scalability.

The QlikView server has the following components:

- **QlikView Directory Service Connector (DSC)**: This keeps track of the users.
- **QlikView Distribution Service**: Publisher effectively extends this functionality if you have it. This is responsible for the reload, distribution, and reduction of QlikView documents.
- **QlikView Management Service (QMS)**: This is the management console, which sends settings to other services.
- **QlikView Server (QVS)**: This hosts the QlikView files and allows user access.
- **QlikView Web Server (QVWS)**: This can be replaced by IIS if required. This is the web server for Access Point and AJAX and is also responsible for load balancing the QVS.

An example of clustered, software load balanced server deployment can be seen in the following diagram:

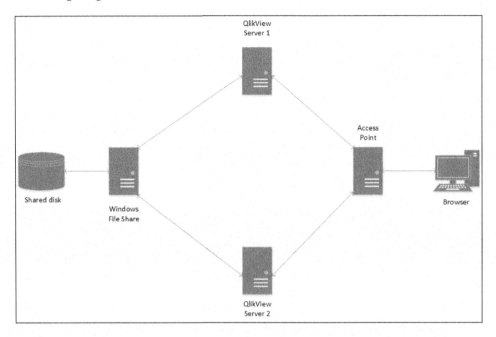

An example of clustered, software load balanced server deployment with clustered Publisher is shown in the following diagram:

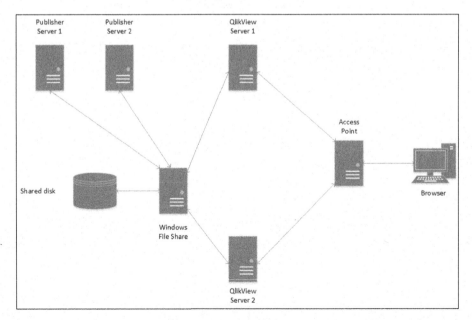

Don't underestimate the importance of this area, especially if yours is an enterprise-level deployment.

QlikView Test Server licenses are available for half the price of full licenses. These are fine for a true test server, but avoid using them for a development server because of the security implications.

Clustering servers enables the construction of very large and scalable environments, and it's straightforward to add extra servers to a cluster. So, if there's the likelihood or requirement to scale out, consider a production cluster from the start.

Bear in mind that the QlikView Server and QlikView Publisher licenses are sold on a per-machine basis. So, the more servers you have, the more licenses you need. This applies to cluster licenses, too—for instance, a three-machine QlikView Server cluster would require a three-node cluster license at three times the cost of a single server license.

Building a reusable, maintainable environment

It's worth spending time getting the environment right at the very start of your implementation. This pays dividends in the long run as it can help reduce errors when moving code between environments.

Background

Whether you have just one QlikView Server or two, three, or more servers, you can make life easier and less error-prone by following a few simple rules right from the start. Most installations have their environments structured along the lines of development, test, and production. These could all either be on one machine or spread across several machines. Moving code between environments commonly causes problems because the environments are inconsistent. Hardcoded paths, differently-spelt folders, and different folder structures all have the potential to cause time-consuming and avoidable errors.

How to do it

Let's use Borchester Models as an example here. The company has been incredibly profitable and has purchased three physical servers and three QlikView Server licenses. The development and test machines are fairly small and run QlikView Small Business Server with a handful of users on each machine. The production machine is much bigger and runs QlikView Enterprise Server. The development machine has two disks and all the QlikView work is done on `D:\`. The test server has only a `C:\` drive, so all the QlikView work resides there. The production server has three drives with the QlikView work residing on `E:\`. The first two developments are underway for `Sales` and `Finance`.

We can immediately see that the hardcoded pathnames need to be changed every time a document is moved between environments. We need to design a solution that ensures that code can be developed, tested, and deployed to production without the need to change it every time it moves between environments.

In this example, we must do two things to ensure that code can be moved easily and without changes. Firstly, the folder structures need to be identical on all three machines, but they don't have to start at the same place on each machine. Secondly, we always use relative paths in our load script.

The folder structures might look something similar to this:

Development machine:

```
D:\
  D:\OtherStuff
  D:\QlikView
    D:\QlikView\Sales (sales.qvw lives here)
      D:\QlikView\Sales\Data
    D:\QlikView\Finance (finance.qvw lives here)
      D:\QlikView\Finance\Data
```

Test machine:

```
C:\
  C:\OtherStuff
  C:\BI
    C:\BI\QlikView
      C:\BI\QlikView\Sales (sales.qvw lives here)
        C:\BI\QlikView\Sales\Data
      C:\BI\QlikView\Finance (finance.qvw lives here)
        C:\BI\QlikView\Finance\Data
```

Production machine:

```
E:\
  E:\OtherStuff
  E:\BI
    E:\BI\Sales (sales.qvw lives here)
      E:\BI\Sales\Data
    E:\BI\Finance (finance.qvw lives here)
      E:\BI\Finance\Data
```

We normally want to have further separation between various file types, so we might consider a more complete structure, such as this:

```
E:\BI\Sales\Includes
E:\BI\Sales\Data\QVD
E:\BI\Sales\Data\Excel
```

In the preceding folder structures, where the QlikView documents reside is different on each machine, but this doesn't matter. As long as they're identical to where the QlikView document resides *downwards*, this will work. Furthermore, if `sales.qvw` needs to access a file called `ForSales.qvd` that resides in `Finance\Data`, we can code the relative path in our script, `[..\Finance\Data\ForSales.qvd]`. Thus, we'll pick up this file no matter which environment we happen to be running in, always assuming the file is there, of course!

There are many variations on this theme. If all the environments were on a single server, we would probably want to use folder permissions and a structure similar to this:

Everything machine:

```
E:\
  E:\BI
  E:\BI\Development
    E:\BI\Development\Sales (sales.qvw lives here)
E:\BI\Development\Sales\Data
    E:\BI\Development\Finance (finance.qvw lives here)
E:\BI\Development\Finance\Data
  E:\OtherStuff
  E:\BI
    E:\BI\Test
      E:\BI\Test\Sales (sales.qvw lives here)
        E:\BI\Test\Sales\Data
      E:\BI\Test\Finance (finance.qvw lives here)
        E:\BI\Test\Finance\Data
```

```
E:\BI\Production
   E:\BI\Production\Sales (sales.qvw lives here)
      E:\BI\Production\Sales\Data
   E:\BI\Production\Finance (finance.qvw lives here)
      E:\BI\Production\Finance\Data
```

Once again, this will work because the relative paths are still the same.

Obviously, this principle can be applied to a PC if that's where you do your development. Things get a little more complicated if the data resides on multiple disks or is not on locally attached storage. We'll discuss solving this with variables in `INCLUDE` files in *Chapter 6, Make It Easy on Yourself–Some QlikView Tips and Tricks*.

It's not uncommon to see folder structures that have a number prefix that gives some sense of sequencing to the folders. Here's an example:

`DocumentName` (for example, `Sales`)

1. **Includes**: These are any `INCLUDE` files needed by any of the QVWs in this application.
2. **Source Data**: This is the original source data; this folder could have subfolders for Excel and text if required.
3. **ETL**: These are all QVWs that convert source data to QVD files. Multiple stages could have the QVWs prefixed by a sequence number.
4. **QVD**: This includes all the files generated in 2.
5. **Application**: `sales.qvw` resides here.
6. **Archive**: This contains old copies of data or documents for reference but is probably best avoided in a production environment.
7. **Documentation**: This includes any specifications or developer notes, along with version control information, such as release notes.

You can devise any kind of folder structure you like to suit your working methods, but the golden rule is to keep it consistent between environments.

QlikView projects need discipline too!

It's tempting to just get coding and respond to verbal requests for additions and improvements, leading to confusion, time, and cost overruns. Avoid the temptation and stay in control.

Background

QlikView is a great tool for iterative development, but it's important to keep track of user requests. Agile development with regular sprints works well for QlikView developments, but the content of each sprint needs to be documented and communicated to your users. It is rare to see large, detailed specifications in QlikView projects. Most requests amount to no more than half a page of text and are often just verbal. Hence, it is necessary to keep track of every enhancement request, problem, and bug, allocating them to sprints as dictated by importance, difficulty, and time required.

How to do it

The most important thing to remember is that, if there's no release discipline with a clear schedule, you will never finish the development. Iterative development means that the user is involved on a regular basis and will always ask for 'just one more thing'. All this will prevent you from drawing a line under each development phase unless you are very clear about development phases and their timings.

There are two ways to approach this problem: either you give the user a list of all the items that will be in a release and provide no more than that list, or you timebox the development. **Timeboxing** means that you start with a list of requirements and priorities, but agree on a period of time in which to do them. If they aren't all done in time, they don't go into the release. Either of these approaches works well with QlikView developments.

Keep track of every change request—even the most trivial ones. This way, you'll be able to tell all your users at once when the request is complete. If you make a simple change while talking with a user or just because it seems like a good idea, you'll either have other users asking when the change will be made or expressing surprise that you have made the change.

Be very clear about what will and won't be in each release. If you use timeboxing for development, your users need to understand that they won't necessarily get everything they expect in each release. Your release notices should itemize what is and isn't in the release.

Depending on how formal your working environment is, you may also need an agreement from a senior user or steering group as to what is to be done. It's also quite likely that they will want to sign off any change before it is actually released to production. The larger the company or project, the greater the chances are that you'll have to comply with these arrangements.

You also need to consider exactly what *release* means in your situation. It could be a release to test, in which case you will concurrently run the test and production releases, and the test release will be the next production release. This requires more careful management as any fixes in the test release would need to be applied to the development release. Alternatively, you might release to test a couple of days before the scheduled release to production, giving the users a little time to test and very little time for any remedial work. This approach means, at the least, that you have only one release at a time to worry about.

Many enterprise environments will most likely have some sort of change management or request tracking system already in place, but it's surprising how many don't. Very large developments may even justify being managed in something similar to Microsoft Project, but this isn't really the right tool for detailed requests. You could, of course, use it to manage your release schedule or a larger ongoing project.

If your project doesn't have a change management or tracking system, create one of your own. It doesn't need to be overly complicated; a spreadsheet will do. Basically, you need to keep a list of requests, snags, and bugs. Note who reported or requested the item and when it was reported, the nature of the issue and who *owns* the issue, the priority or severity of the issue, its progress, outcome, and outcome date (or release), and who completed the task. From this, you can keep track of every item.

Even a simple tracking system is better than no tracking system at all. Don't rely on e-mails and water cooler conversations; log everything in your tracking system. If it isn't in the tracking system, it doesn't happen.

You could even create a small QlikView application that uses your spreadsheet to allow management to see how productive you have been!

Can you deliver?

Well, of course you can deliver; you're a QlikView professional! However, not every project proposal is sensible, so take the time to review any project proposal carefully.

Background

Before embarking on any QlikView project, always ask a question: "Does this make sense?" As QlikView is so powerful and it's so easy to import data, it's also very easy to assume that anything is possible. However, possible isn't always sensible, so there are several other basic questions to be asked. Is the data to be analyzed actually available and accessible? What form is the data in? How about data quality? How much effort will be involved in developing the solution? What value or benefit can be delivered to the user if this development is undertaken?

How to do it

If you have ever done any kind of systems or business analysis, you must realize that all these questions—and more—are basics and not applicable only to QlikView. However, QlikView does tend to highlight problems and issues sooner than you might expect, mostly because it is so quick to develop a basic data model.

Data availability is a good starting point. It is surprisingly common for a user to ask for something that can't be done, simply because there is no data or no means of getting the data. One example of this we've encountered is when a client told us, "We want to chart all our sales against those of our competitors". Well, getting *our* sales figures shouldn't be too hard, but it's highly unlikely that the competitors will hand over that kind of information willingly.

Data accessibility is a different matter. Within your own organization, you should be able to get the data you need, though there may, of course, be restrictions on its use. However, there may be some data that lies outside your organization that you can use. Typical examples are government websites, where all kinds of useful data can be obtained and it's perfectly possible to grab tables of data from public websites. You should watch out for any copyright or reuse restrictions, though.

The form data takes is critical. Pulling data from database tables is usually very straightforward, and as a general rule, a database in your organization's environment should be reliably up-to-date. Spreadsheets are a different matter though. They're very easy to pull into QlikView, and there are some excellent tools to manipulate content, but pulling in many spreadsheets should raise concerns. Firstly, unless there is iron discipline around their maintenance, they can easily be out of date or not match the other data for timing reasons. Secondly, any spreadsheet under user control can have columns added or removed or its name changed, usually with unexpected or even disastrous results. Thirdly, by their very nature, there will always be some manual process involved in their use. Something as simple as the user forgetting to drop a spreadsheet into a folder at the correct time could lead to strange results or a load failure.

A fourth concern about spreadsheets is data quality. Most spreadsheets have little or no enforcement to ensure that the data in them is clean. Date fields can't always be relied on to contain dates, and so on. The same can be said of databases, but database data tends to be of better quality and more reliable as a rule.

Try to ensure that all the data required for your development arrives on time, in the right place, and consistent in quality. The more spreadsheets required, the louder the alarm bells should ring. If you absolutely have to have lots of spreadsheets, ensure that you do as much as you can in the load script to validate them. Never assume that just because the spreadsheet is there and you can open it, it's the right one. The import file wizard has some great features to help you manipulate spreadsheet data.

We discuss dirty data and some ways of fixing it in *Chapter 4, It's All About Understanding the Data*.

Having established where all the data is coming from and what the user is asking for, how long does it take to develop the solution? Unfortunately, we can't help you with that. Experience will be your guide, and in the words of *Stephen Redmond*, "There is no substitute for experience".

Finally, what value will be delivered as a result of this solution? Value can mean many things and depends on the context. The solution could mean that your company can identify which products lose money, save someone a day a week preparing a report, or discover that more people are *sick* when there's an important football match on TV. All these things have some value, but it will be for you, and most likely your users, to decide whether there is sufficient value to make the project worthwhile.

Summary

In this chapter, you learned about the importance of the infrastructure for a QlikView deployment and some ideas about the architectures that can be employed as the size of deployment grows. We looked at some options to make our environment reusable and maintainable by designing the folder structure correctly.

You also learned some general principles about discipline that can be applied to a QlikView project to ensure that development phases do not overrun.

Finally, we considered some aspects that affect the feasibility of a project, paying particular attention to data quality and availability.

2
Building the Correct Environment

In this chapter, we will cover the following keys:

- Creating and enforcing site standards
- Designing a site-style template
- Making document names meaningful
- Separation of responsibilities, change management, and thinking about security
- Understanding different environments

Creating and enforcing site standards

Users like applications that behave consistently and have a standard look and feel. You can achieve this by creating and enforcing site development standards.

Background

It's always a good idea to set some rules for how applications should be developed, regardless of the tool you are using for development. A clear, sensible set of standards that everyone can agree on should be developed before starting any major development. By thinking things through carefully beforehand, you will find that once you create your site standards, you probably never need to change them. Generally, your standards should include details such as change documentation (refer to the section, *Separation of responsibilities, change management, and thinking about security*, in this chapter), coding standards, naming conventions, screen layouts, and styling (refer to *Designing a site-style template* in this chapter).

How to do it

Site standards really fall into two areas: the part the user doesn't see (such as the script) and the part he/she does see (the GUI). This section is concerned with the part that the user does not see.

Plan and create your site standards as a small project. Take inputs from the whole development team, and create standards that everyone is comfortable with. To ensure that everyone sticks to the rules, consider having code reviews from time to time, where peers review one another's code. Even the threat of code reviews tends to raise standards as a whole. Alternatively, always have a peer review of each new application or change. Not only does this help keep standards high, but developers will also learn from each other. A further benefit is that there is a deeper understanding of each application within the developer group as a result.

Site standards can be as brief as you prefer. In fact, you can probably set out everything you need in two or three pages. The more pages, the less likely the standards will be adhered to; so, try to keep the standards brief and sensible.

Enforce the standards rigorously. If the development team has agreed to them, it has no excuse not to adhere to them.

Site standards will vary from place to place, but let's discuss a few things to consider when creating yours.

The script is where a lot of the work happens, and it is worth ensuring that as much precalculation as possible is done there. This will help improve the GUI's performance as QlikView will not need to calculate the same thing over and over again. We will discuss this in detail in *Chapter 6, Make It Easy on Yourself – Some QlikView Tips and Tricks*.

Always break the script into several tabs, ideally one per input file or table. Keep comments at the top of each tab to explain what it does, unless its function is already very clear or trivial. This improves readability and makes it easier to alter the order in which things are done. Make one tab an exit tab, containing just an `EXIT SCRIPT;` statement. You can then move this tab backward and forward while debugging to save reading in every table.

QlikView is very flexible about naming variables, but it's best to follow a convention as it is easier to search through code when you know that variables always have some standard prefix characteristic. For this reason, consider using something similar to `vName`, `varName`, or `VarName` as a standard. You don't need to use variations of `v` or `var`, of course—anything will do as long as it's consistent and not confused with column names. Note that QlikView does not let you use a number as the first character of a variable's name.

Expressions are a powerful part of QlikView, and it is very common to use the same expression in many places in the same or similar applications. If you find that any expression is used more than once, you should seriously consider storing it in a variable. This will help avoid problems where the *same* expression gives two (or more) different answers.

Still on the subject of variables, we recommend that they be always created in the script. It is, of course, possible to create them in **Settings | Variable Overview**, but this approach always seems to be a bit muddled. Variables from the script and input that goes directly into **Variable Overview** all appear here, and it's impossible to tell where the variable was actually created. If you always create variables in the script or in INCLUDE files, you can search for them much more easily.

If you have many variables to be used in several applications, consider placing them in one or more INCLUDE files. This is especially important if you have expressions to reuse and also if you use binary loads. Binary loads do not inherit variables from the loaded QVW file. INCLUDE files are also extremely useful because a change to be applied to every application can be made in just one place. So, for instance, if you wanted to change the thousands separator (the first line of a default script) and if it was in an INCLUDE file, a single one-line change would cover all your applications. In fact, we recommend putting all the defaults that QlikView generates at the top of the script into a site-wide INCLUDE file.

In the script itself, consider using version numbers and possibly version dates—this is not the same thing as a reload date. You could, for example, use the version number and date on an opening screen to inform the user (and yourself). Alternatively, you could put this information in the changes spreadsheet we mentioned in *Chapter 1, Behind Every Successful Project Is a Plan*, in the section *QlikView projects need discipline too!* and load it in with the script.

One common complaint from users when they see an application in **Access Point** is that they don't always recognize it because the thumbnail image keeps changing. This is because the image shown in **Access Point** is of the tab showing the last save done by the developer. Before deploying an application, always save it at the tab you want displayed on **Access Point**. This is not the same as forcing QlikView to always show the same sheet on startup. You can send the user to a completely different tab when opening the document by setting a trigger—**Open Document Properties | Triggers | On Open**—and creating an action to open a specific sheet.

Building the Correct Environment

In the following example, we want **Opening Sheet (SH01)**, as in this image, to always be shown first:

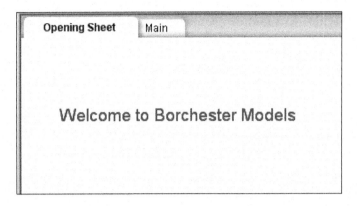

For this, you can do the following:

1. Select **Settings | Document Properties | Triggers** and choose **OnOpen** from the **Document Event Triggers** box. Click on **Add Action(s)**:

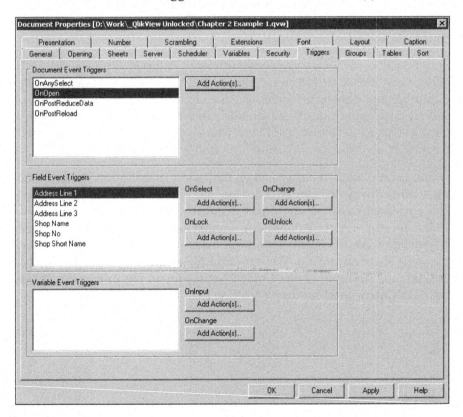

2. Click on **Add** in the **Actions** tab, and in the **Add Action** box, click on **Layout** under **Action Type** and **Activate Sheet** under **Action**. Then, click on **OK**:

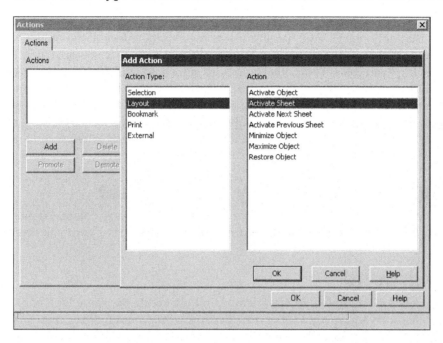

3. Enter the sheet name in the **Sheet ID** box and click on **OK**:

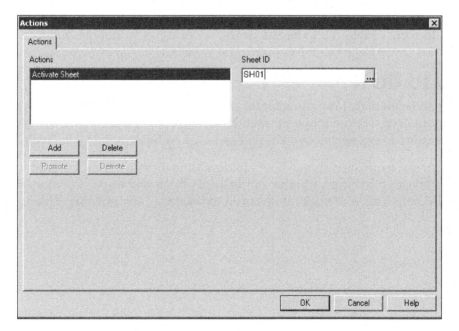

4. Click on **OK** once more to confirm the change. Now, every time the document is opened, it will automatically start with this sheet, and a thumbnail of the sheet will appear on **Access Point**.

It is said that only one COBOL program was ever written and all the others were copied from that one. The same may be true of QlikView, so it is worth mentioning the following even if it isn't strictly to do with site standards. If you copy an existing document to use as the basis for a new application, beware that all groups and variables will also be copied with it. Take the time to review and discard those that are not needed. In fact, we would probably discard all the variables because if you follow the ideas set out previously, you'll load what you need in the script anyway.

Designing a site-style template

To help achieve a consistent look and feel to your applications, create a site-style template. This is a small QlikView document that forms part of your site standards.

Background

Having a site-style template to work from can help create the same look and feel for your applications and saves a lot of time because you do not have to create every new application from scratch. Your site-style template includes your corporate color scheme, logos, and prototypes for objects. It can also include a framework script that names the standard `INCLUDE` files. A site-style template has advantages over the theme maker, which is accessible from **Document properties** | **Layout**, because this feature does not enable you to include logos, scripting, or prototypes of objects.

How to do it

The site-style template forms an integral part of your site's standards. Rather than spelling out every feature in the site standards, by creating a template, you can set the style rules. Every new document will be based on the template you create.

Creating a site template can save hours of development effort later, especially if all your screens need to have a number of identical objects and a specific color scheme. It can also help if all your applications need to have a similar opening screen.

The script could consist of four tabs: the first one has a framework for the change history. It could load a documentation spreadsheet if you choose to do your documentation this way. The second tab names any standard INCLUDE files you use. The third can be an empty tab, intended as a placeholder for the first file to be loaded, and the fourth tab is the **EXIT SCRIPT** tab, which we mentioned before:

The next step is to create a standard screen. Different applications have different layout requirements—for instance, you may have many selectors in one application and very few in another. The idea here is to just create things that are common to all applications. This may be the background color, a logo, and possibly a Current Selections object. You may also need to consider the screen sizes that your application will be used on. You can set some guidelines by creating horizontal and vertical line objects and positioning them at the extremities of the useable space, as shown in the following screenshot.

The caption settings for a vertical line that defines the right hand limit of a 1,024x768 screen layout are as follows:

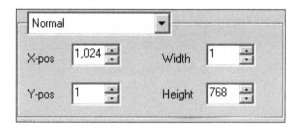

Some sites have color schemes specific to each application area, so if you have multiple application areas and each application comprises several QlikView documents, you can create a template for each application area.

Setting the default colors for objects is an important step that can save plenty of time. The easiest way to do this is to change the properties of the `Current Selections` object. Typically, you will probably change the colors for **Active Caption** and **Inactive Caption** as follows:

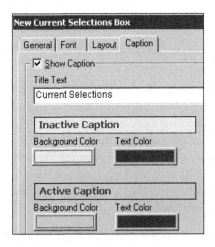

You can change the borders, if you use them at all:

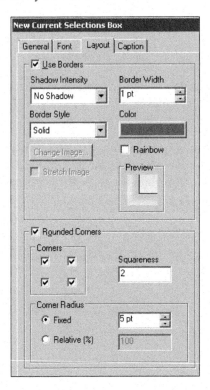

There are also several options that you can select from by navigating to **Settings | Document Properties | General** to customize screen objects, as shown in the following image:

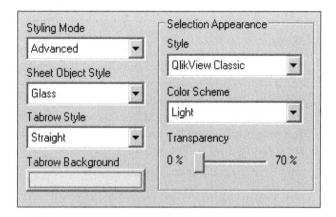

You can achieve some subtle changes by playing around with these features; in particular, the **Selection Appearance** setting can be changed to make multiple selections easier using Windows checkboxes; for example, take a look at this listbox:

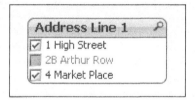

In order to make multiple noncontiguous selections, it isn't necessary to hold down the *Ctrl* key in the preceding example.

Having created an object with default colors and styling, you can easily use the paint brush feature to apply these attributes to any other object you create.

You can take the template design even further if you wish. For instance, you could create a bar chart object with a calculated dimension of 1, and an expression of 1. Then, you would be able to set your color preferences in **Chart Properties | Colours** and use this chart as the basis for another.

Try to maintain a consistent approach for the items that are harder to template because they vary from document to document. That is, try to have long selector lists down to the left of the screen and short selectors and ribbons (for example, dates) across the top of the screen. Avoid putting selectors on the right-hand side or along the bottom of the screen as having to use a scroll bar to get to them would very quickly annoy most users.

Finally, consider whether to use the minimize/maximize feature that is available with each chart type. Sometimes, this feature can make your screens look a bit ugly, so it is worth using a button instead to toggle the visibility of charts and other objects. If you do go for the button idea, remember to create a default button, its trigger, and a chart that responds to the button. Don't forget to disable minimize/maximize in the chart by navigating to **Properties | Caption**:

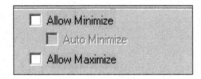

Making document names meaningful

Most developers keep several versions of a QlikView document and prefix or suffix them with a date or version number. Deploying differently-named versions of the same application to the **Access Point** should be avoided.

Background

There is nothing to prevent a developer from deploying many differently-named versions of an application to the **Access Point**. It's also possible to deploy different versions of a document with the same name to the **Access Point** by putting them in different mount folders.

Obviously, these situations should be avoided as they lead to confusion. Always deploy the same document with the same name as part of standard practice, use version numbering in code, and display it for the user to see in the document itself, as described in the *Creating and enforcing site standards* section in this chapter.

How to do it

As developers, we all like to keep a few different versions of a QlikView document in case we need to go back to a previous version. Everyone has their own way of assigning version numbers—dates, numbers, letters, children's names, and so on. However, the version that is deployed to the **Access Point** should only ever be the application name agreed upon. By all means, use whatever works for you as a developer in terms of naming the various versions of a document in your development area, but remember that numbers tend to work best. However, you should agree on the deployed document name with your users, designer, business analyst, or whoever has overall responsibility for the development. Never name documents just in capitals as it's confusing to see names in capitals in QMC.

There can, of course, be exceptions to a rule; one circumstance could be where you have the test and production environments on the same server. In this case, the current testing version and current production version of an application, although in separate folders, will both appear in the **Access Point**. The only way around this is to prefix the test version name with **TEST** or something else that clearly indicates its purpose. When deploying to production, obviously, the prefix should be removed.

Always deploy a document with the same name to the **Access Point** at every stage. Using different names would just confuse users. Using multiple names for the same document also means that you can *lose* QlikView licenses. This is surprisingly easy to do.

Suppose you deploy **TEST Sales Dashboard** to the **Access Point** and allocate five CALs to it. Your users test the document and declare it ready to go live. You move **TEST Sales Dashboard** to the appropriate production folder and rename it `Sales Dashboard`. Then, you delete **TEST Sales Dashboard** from the test folder. By doing this, you have just *lost* the five licenses allocated to it.

You may see something similar to this in QMC before moving the document:

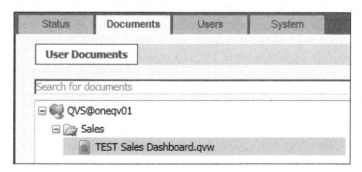

You'll see something similar to this if you delete or move the document:

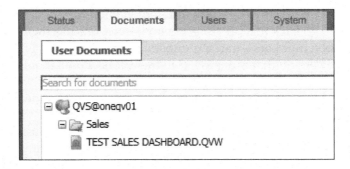

This is a very common problem, but it is fairly easy to fix. The key to it is releasing the licenses in QMC *before* deleting the document. However, if the licenses are not released before the deletion, there are two ways to fix the problem:

- Create a dummy document with the same name as the deleted document in the folder that it was deleted from. It can be any QlikView document as long as the name is the same. Then, go ahead and release the licenses and delete the dummy document.
- There's a last resort option, and this is to clear the QlikView license in the QMC and reinput it. This is a drastic option, though, as it would release all your document licenses, so exercise extreme caution. Ideally, make a note of each document and how many licenses are allocated to it before clearing the server license. For large deployments, you really want to avoid this if you can.

Separation of responsibilities, change management, and thinking about security

Developing an application can be a single person task, but more often, there are more people involved. Change requests and access to the application need to be controlled. It is also important to consider what kind of security is required.

Background

If you are in the enviable position of being able to develop an application from scratch on your own, you don't have to worry about the separation of tasks. Change management is a lot easier too, but there are still aspects that need to be considered.

How to do it

You have probably come across the question, "How do you eat an elephant?" to which the answer is, "Cut it into small chunks and eat it bit by bit". The same is true when developing a QlikView application. The advantage of having all these small bits is that different people can work on the application at the same time.

However, in reality, there are only a couple of tasks that can be divided easily. Having one person working on the data model and another working on the GUI is the ideal split of labor on a larger development without causing too much confusion.

Ensure that there are defined roles and establish who is responsible for controlling common items, such as variables and module code.

On complex systems where a lot of tables need to be created, data gathering and ETL can be broken down further and worked on separately; however, this is an exception rather than the rule.

Having more than one person working on the GUI layer is a lot more complicated and prone to problems. It is possible for different people to use the same data model through a binary load and for each to then work on his/her own tab. However, a procedure needs to be in place to handle the addition or modification of variables and changes to the document's settings.

If you are using module code (VBScript or JScript functions and subroutines), this will add to the complication as it is held in one place for the whole document. Therefore, it can become disjointed if more than one person modifies it.

If you have taken the approach of having multiple people developing the GUI, someone will have to shoulder responsibility for taking the separate documents containing relevant tabs and pulling them together into the completed GUI.

Luckily, QlikView has a few tricks that make this easier:

1. Open the master document in one instance of QlikView, create a new tab, and then open one of the separate documents in another instance.
2. Press *Ctrl* + *Shift* + *S* on the tab to be copied to make all hidden objects visible.
3. Rubber band all the objects (by hold-left-click and dragging a box around them) and copy them to the clipboard.
4. Move to the master document and paste the objects. Note that hidden objects will not be visible on the master document unless the appropriate conditions are met.

This can be done for each separate document.

This brings us to the next question: how do we handle change requests?

QlikView does have a mechanism to integrate version control systems, but this is difficult to set up. Be very careful about using version control systems with QlikView. Most are unwieldy and have weaknesses that can easily be exploited. You can add the `-prj` directory structure to the version control system to monitor and control changes to objects and document properties. This works well enough for large, complex applications but is too unwieldy for most.

The simplest approach is to ensure that all changes are well commented in the script. A simple "When, Who, and What" indication will help future developers understand the history. Changes to the GUI layer could be shown on a separate *changes* sheet in the GUI as useful information for the user.

Another approach is to keep a spreadsheet of changes made for each application. This only needs to be very simple, with perhaps the version number, date, who changed, and what was changed. This can be stored in the `9. Documentation` subfolder (refer to *Chapter 1, Behind Every Successful Project Is a Plan*) and then read into your application so that a change log can be shown to the user.

Be sure to have a release structure, as mentioned in *Chapter 1, Behind Every Successful Project Is a Plan* as the temptation to keep tinkering can be too great. We all want to produce something to be proud of and give the end user as much information as we possibly can, but we also want to be able to say "It's finished".

In our view, the last stage of developing an application is security. Although it is the last to be done, it should be in the design phase from the very beginning.

There are a number of ways that a document can be secured, each with its advantages, but they can be broken down basically into four main types:

- Filesystem access, where network permissions dictate who can open a document
- QlikView's authentication, via QMC (Enterprise server only)
- Document license; whoever has a document license can open it
- Section access, with users coded into the document (with or without data reduction)

Decide on the security model you want to implement as this can have a major effect on your design model, especially if you plan to add **Data Reduction**.

In *Chapter 8*, *To Deployment and Beyond* we will cover security in more detail, including the pitfalls of using Section Access and how to avoid them.

Understanding the differences in environments

QlikView comes in many shapes and sizes and with extra add-ons too. These can have a dramatic effect on how your server is configured. In addition, there are many ways that you can license the use of your documents. All have their advantages, and all have cost implications.

Background

How your server runs depends on the basic server version you are using. It could be Small Business Server, Enterprise Server, or Extranet Server. You need to know whether it is a Full license or a Test license and whether QlikView Publisher is installed and licensed.

Once the server type is established, next come User Licenses (sometimes referred to as CALs). There are currently four types to choose from: Named User, Document, Session, and Usage.

How to do it

Should we use Small Business Edition or Enterprise Edition?

There are a couple of significant differences between these two versions. Firstly, the number of User CALs that Small Business Edition can have is limited to 100 Document CALs and 25 Named CALs. Secondly, you can only secure access to documents using NTFS on Small Business Edition. QlikView's own DMS Authentication document level security along with NTFS is available on Enterprise Edition.

One of the fundamental settings of QlikView Server is on one of the configuration tabs as a simple radio button choice. Under **Authorization** on the **Security** tab, you have the choice of either **NTFS** or **DMS** (Small Business Edition users only have NTFS):

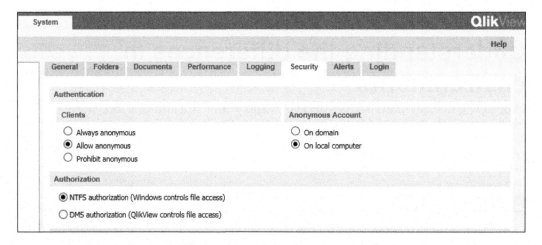

With **NTFS**, you rely on Windows file level security to control who can view this document once the CAL licenses and Section Access controls have been applied. This is the default option and works well in most installations as Active Directory groups can be used to control access to specific documents.

If you need to control authorization to documents and do not have filesystem administrator rights as the QlikView Server administrator, you may need to consider DMS. DMS allows control of authorization without administrator rights and makes QMC a single point of reference for control.

You cannot mix and match these options for different documents; it is one or the other for the whole system. Changing this during the life of the server can be a long process as each and every QlikView document would need to have the authorization options reset, either within the filesystem (if **NTFS** is selected) or within QMC Task Management (if **DMS** is selected).

With or without Publisher?

One of the major add-ons to QlikView is Publisher, which, among other things, allows documents to be refreshed and distributed via e-mail to individuals with optional data reduction applied to each variation. This is known as **Loop and Reduce**, but you should think carefully about how many different variations of the document will be produced, as many versions will greatly extend the processing time required.

When a Publisher license is activated, it has a major impact on your installation; it not only adds extra functionality to **Task Management**, but also alters the way documents are handled on the server.

Without Publisher, QlikView Server stores a single copy of your document (`.QVW`), which is refreshed periodically and viewed on the server (using Access Point) from the same physical file.

With Publisher installed, you now have a "Source" and a "User" area. You place your QVW document in the "Source" area and QlikView Server will refresh it when invoked and update this file, but will then distribute it to the "User" area, where it becomes available to the end user (using the **Access Point**). Files in the "Source" area are not accessible from the **Access Point**.

This is very helpful when your QlikView application has many data gathering and ETL documents, as none of these would be distributed to the "User" area and are therefore hidden from view.

Another major feature with Publisher is the ability to have multiple triggers on document refreshes; whereas, without Publisher, you can only have a single trigger. So, with Publisher, you can have a timed refresh, an EDX-based (External trigger) refresh, and a refresh upon the completion of another document, if you so wish.

Do you need Publisher? This not just adds functionality, but is also a major structure change. In some cases, the different way of handling files and the ability to have multiple triggers is a good enough reason to use it, even if you are never going to e-mail reports or variations of a document.

There is one thing to consider with Publisher: once licensed, you cannot take it off without completely reinstalling the server from scratch.

Do you need a Test server? Qlik offers a Test server license (at a cost), which has the same license model as your main server. This allows you to create an identical server for development and testing. As with most good things, there are some drawbacks; firstly, you cannot lease a named license from a Test server, and secondly, the word "test" is placed as a watermark on all graphs and charts when accessed via Access Point. As you cannot lease a named license from a Test server, we would always recommend that it be used only for test and never for development.

Does your budget stretch to a Test server? This is ideal to manage controlled releases as a development version can be tested without affecting the production version.

QlikView has a wide variation in document CALs. Basically, there are four types, and each has its advantages and cost implications. You are not limited to one type of license on your server; in fact, you could have them all if you require. The four types are:

- **Named User**: Here, one user has access to as many documents as required. It is typically used for developers and power users. Currently, Named User CALs are almost four times the cost of a Document CAL, so if a user needs access to four or more documents, it is usually more cost effective to assign this user to a Named User CAL rather than four or more individual Document CALs.
- **Document**: Here, one user has access to one document for as much time as he/she needs. It is most cost effective when a user only needs access to up to three documents.
- **Session**: Here, many users have access to any one document, but only one user has access at a time. Sessions CALs are very expensive, so you need to think carefully about usage patterns before employing this type of license.
- **Usage**: One user has access to one document for 60 minutes in a month. If you have users who only access a document for a short period of time, maybe to view the monthly sales figures when they are published, a Usage CAL may be a good solution.

A typical server is made up of Document and Named User CALs as these are most popular and cost effective for normal use, whereas Session and Usage CALs are more suited to larger implementations. Session CALs are a good solution for a large, anonymous audience.

Summary

In this chapter, you learned about the importance of creating and enforcing standards for coding and layout. We also discovered that proper discipline about naming QlikView documents will make things much easier for users, and licenses will not mysteriously disappear from the server.

We also discussed the separation of responsibilities, change management, and that we need to consider security early in our development journey, not right at the end.

Finally, we looked at the different server and client license types and learned about the characteristics of each.

3
Are You Sitting Comfortably? Be More Productive

In this chapter, we will cover the following key topics:

- A bit more about license types
- Making yourself comfortable and productive
- Never lose your work
- Some useful global settings
- Some best practices for developers
- Hidden features – Easter eggs
- A few do's and don'ts

A bit more about license types

Qlik provides several ways of licensing the desktop version for developers. In this section, we'll explain the differences and what you as a developer should be aware of.

Background

From a developer's point of view, there are three types of license that will enable you to create and modify QlikView documents. However, only two of them are useful once you pass the initial experimentation stage. The three types we will review here are Personal Edition, Stand Alone (Local Client), and Leased License (Named User).

How to do it

Qlik encourages potential users to try out QlikView by allowing anyone to download a free copy of Personal Edition. This is a full-featured development environment, but its usage is restricted to documents created with this copy of the software along with a handful of QlikView demonstration documents. This means that it is only of use in an environment where you are both the sole developer and user. However, Personal Edition can be upgraded to a full Local Client developer version on the payment of a fee.

To use QlikView for any corporate or collaborative development, you need either a Local Client or Named User license.

The Local Client version is completely unrestricted in that QlikView documents can be modified or created with it and deployed to internal or external users or customers. If you are a freelance developer, this is probably the version you want, unless you can afford to step up to a server version with Named User licenses.

 One area that can cause some confusion is upgrading Personal Edition to Local Client.

The **Help** menu has an item called **License Update**, which might lead you to think that this is where to input the license key that you are provided with if you pay to upgrade. In fact, this is completely the wrong place and to input your license key you need to click on **Settings | User Preferences** and then on the **License** tab. Clicking on the **Change** button will bring up a window where you can input your license key and control number:

Chapter 3

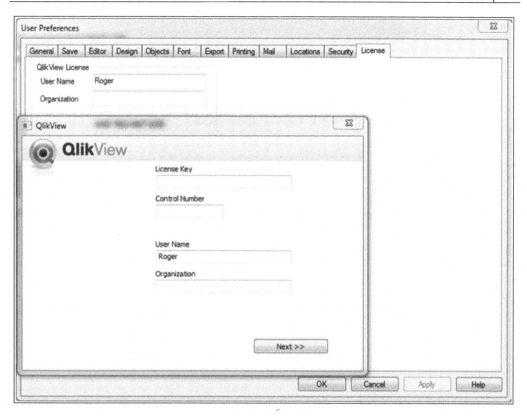

Finally, in most corporate environments, you will most likely lease a Named User license locally from QlikView Server. This is done by installing Personal Edition on your PC and then connecting to QlikView Server, where you are granted a Named User license, and opening a document there. This effectively means that your Personal Edition version becomes a Local Client desktop developer's version. Note that you cannot be granted a license from a Test server; it must be a "full" server, which is Small Business or Enterprise Server.

To verify that you are leasing a license from a particular server, go to QlikView **Start Page**. Under **Resources**, there is an item called **License information**. Clicking on this brings up a **License information** panel similar to that shown in the following screenshot:

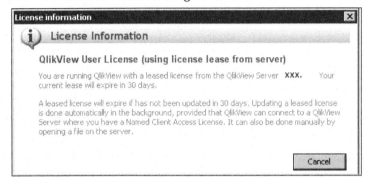

Note that in versions prior to QlikView v11.2 SR7, the license details are shown at the top of the **Start Page** screen.

Remember that you need to reconnect to the server at least once in every 30 days in order to renew your license. As long as your desktop version has access to the server, this will happen automatically, and you will not need to open the server connection window.

Make yourself comfortable and productive

It's all too easy to just start using the developer environment without really thinking about how to make it work best for yourself.

Background

Before starting on a new development, especially with a new installation of the developer environment, spend a few minutes setting things up to suit your own style and development needs. Simple things such as having more recent items in your start menu can save time as you would not have to navigate your way to a document every time you need to open it. Here, we will explore a few of our favorite settings, all of which can save a little time here and there, making you comfortable and more productive.

It's surprising how much difference a few little adjustments to the developer environment can make to productivity, but don't forget that you want your users to be productive too!

How to do it

You can perform the following steps for this. All the settings in this section can be found in **Settings | User Preferences**, on the **General** tab:

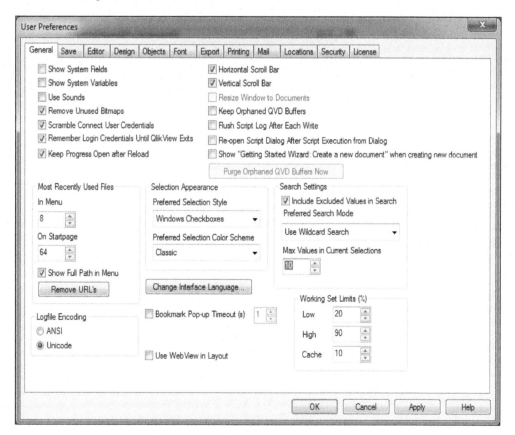

Most recently used files

If you are working on a lot of QVWs in a deployment—for instance, many QVD builders—change the value in **In Menu** to a more suitable number. This will increase the number of files shown in the list at the bottom of the **File** menu. The default **On Startpage** value is probably enough for most purposes, but we often make these two values match. Finally, always select the **Show Full Path in Menu** option. It does what it says; so, rather than showing a file path containing ellipses (…) to the QVWs, it shows the whole path. This is very useful when you have various versions of a QVW in different folders as it makes it much easier to select the correct one.

Selection appearance

Perhaps more of a styling option than a developer's choice, this is nevertheless a handy feature. By default, QlikView presents data in a listbox without any kind of checkbox, so making individual selections requires the user to hold the *Ctrl* key while selecting. Using one of the other options, such as **Windows Checkboxes** means that the *Ctrl* key doesn't have to be used; individual selections can simply be ticked. If you have a long list of values, you and your users may prefer to use a checkboxes option:

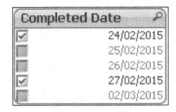

Search settings

Although there are several options in search settings, in our opinion, the only one that you need 99 percent of the time is wildcard search. Using this option opens a search box with two asterisks (**) with the cursor between them. Users always search with partial data, so we don't see why you would use normal search, which requires an exact match. On rare occasions, you might use fuzzy search, but wildcard search covers almost every eventuality. Note that fuzzy search can't be set from the **General** tab but from within a search object. The *desktop help* incorrectly indicates that fuzzy search is an option in the **General** tab (as at QlikView v11.2 SR9).

Max values in current selections

This is another option that arguably has more to do with styling but can make development easier. Selecting a higher number has the effect of changing the display in the **Current Selections** box. By default, QlikView shows the selections of a field as, for example, A1, A2, or A3. Once the threshold of **Max Values** in **Current Selections** is exceeded, the **Current Selections** box shows something similar to "7 of 290", rather than the actual selected values. By increasing the value of **Max Values** in **Current Selections**, more actual values are shown. A slight downside is that this might very quickly take up all the space in the **Current Selections** box, so take care if you have fields with long values in them. It's worth pointing out that this setting does not affect the `GetCurrentSelections()` function, but you can pass this a parameter to get the same effect.

Never lose your work

It's happened to all of us. Change the script and reload the document…and the script fails, wiping out all your changes.

Background

For those of you who already write QlikView script, how many times have you made changes to the script and reloaded, only to find that there is an error and the reload has stopped? The document is cancelled and reloaded to an old state, losing your most recent changes. To prevent this annoying problem, there is a simple user setting you can make.

How to do it

Here's what you can do. Select **User Preferences** from the **Settings** menu and click on the **Save** tab. Look for the **Save Before Reload** checkbox and select it. This will save all your changes before the script reloads, and they will still be there even if the script fails:

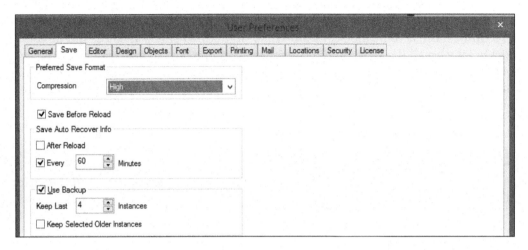

There are a couple of extra options you may want to set here as well.

Save Auto Recover Info performs an auto save every x minutes in a temporary file. Should your system crash, you will at least have a copy at the saved point. We recommend that you set this option to every 60 minutes or less. Bear in mind that while the save takes place, the developer system will be unresponsive; for large applications, this could be a minute or more. Balance the frequency of saves against the time it takes to do them.

The other option is **Use Backup** with the **Keep Last x Instances** option. Upon setting this, QlikView will automatically keep the last x number of QVWs. Every time you do a save (or reload, if **Save Before Reload** is selected), QlikView saves the current QVW, prefixing the name with "Version x of ......" and incrementing the x value with each new save. The current document is then saved as normal. If there are now more than x version files on your system, the oldest one will be deleted to ensure that only x versions of the files remain. Setting this value to 4 or 5 is about right in our opinion.

Having several instances of backups can be very useful. Sometimes, changes just don't do what is expected, so having the ability to get back to an earlier version of your code can get you out of a hole.

We all make mistakes in the script, so when the script fails and the reload is cancelled, losing lots of changes is frustrating and time-consuming. At the minimum, always have **Save Before Reload** selected—it will save lots of time and frustration when the inevitable happens.

Some useful global settings

There are a handful of user settings that, by default, are turned off but are so useful, it makes us wonder why they aren't just permanently turned on.

Background

There are certain design options that need to be turned on in order to get the best from the developer's workbench. These turn on extended features that allow custom formatting of cells, extended styling options such as rounded corners on objects, and debugging problems after deploying your document to a server. When a QVW fails on a server, the log file can be quite unhelpful, but one simple setting before deployment will help you find problems quickly.

How to do it

Select **User Preferences** from the **Settings** menu and then click on the **Design** tab. There are three options here that should be set in order to use the workbench more effectively.

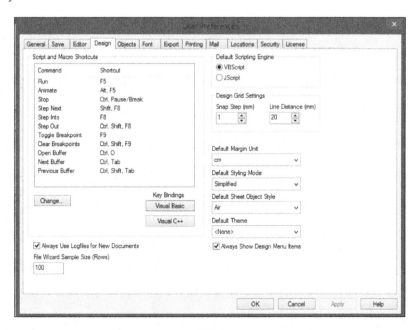

Default Styling Mode

Firstly, look for **Default Styling Mode** on the right-hand side, and change it from **Simplified** to **Advanced**. The effect of this will be to turn on various features in the **Layout** tab of an object's properties.

Chart Properties with **Default Styling Mode** set to **Simplified** is shown in the following screenshot:

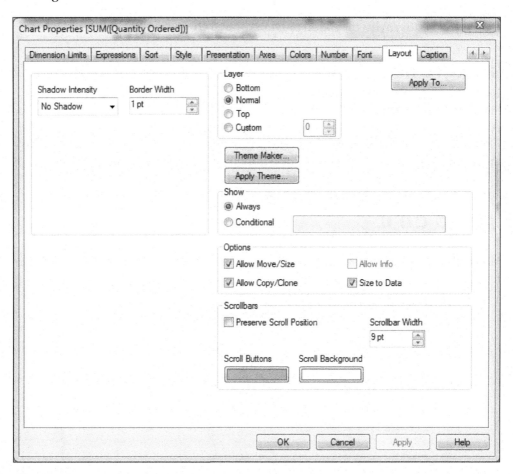

Chart Properties with **Default Styling Mode** set to **Advanced** is shown in the following screenshot:

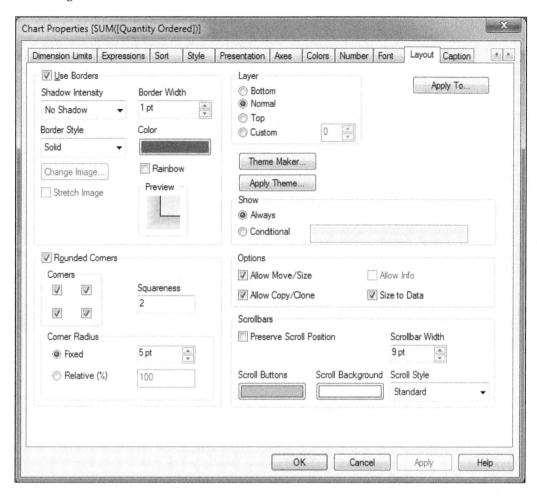

You can also turn on **Advanced Styling Mode** via **Settings | Document Properties | General** for individual documents.

Always Use Logfiles for New Documents

This option turns the **Generate Log File** option on in **Document Properties** whenever you create a new document. The log file is a very useful debugging tool when your document is deployed to a server. It is the ideal place to start looking when a document fails to reload on the server as it shows you exactly where in the script it failed and what the error was. The only drawback is that you still can't see what happened if the failure occurred in a hidden script.

Selecting **Always Use Logfiles for New Documents** in **Settings | User Preferences | Design** saves you the trouble of remembering to select **Generate Logfile** in the **General** tab of **Document Properties**. You'll always have a logfile available to help debug failures.

Always Show Design Menu Items

With this option selected, the presentation of straight and pivot tables can be altered. For example, you can change the default colors of a column, the thickness of the divider lines, or even the column header's display properties.

Once this option is selected, right-click anywhere over a straight or pivot table, and you will see an extra menu item, **Custom Format Cell**. This appears beneath the existing **Equal Column Width** option. Click on **Custom Format Cell** and a new properties box will appear:

Here, you can change the appearance of a table in ways you can't in the normal properties window:

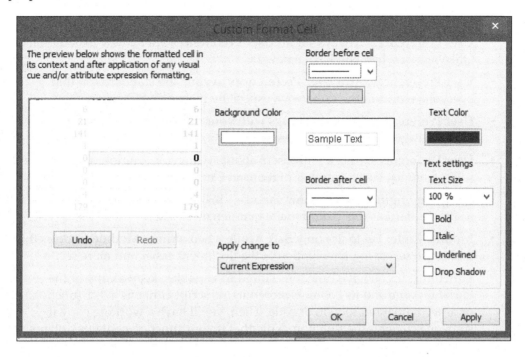

Some best practices for developers

It's preferable to always do things in a consistent manner, both personally and as part of a team. There are many ways to set up the QlikView environment, and if each developer chooses his own settings, this can lead to all kinds of issues and inconsistencies when you start to assemble a system.

Background

You might consider using some of the following ideas as part of your site standards. In any event, they're all good habits to get into. As they are all self-explanatory, we will present them as bullet points.

How to do it

- **User Preferences**: Always set up **User Preferences** the same on each machine you use.
- **User Preferences**: Always set up **User Preferences** after a new installation of QlikView or when you have a new PC.
- **User Preferences**: Add **User Preferences** to your site standards so that everyone works in the same way, especially if sharing PCs or a server.
- **User Preferences**: Review settings with your whole team to ensure that everyone agrees with the choices made.
- **User Preferences**: Check with users about styling; for example, checkboxes to select from list boxes, number of items in **Current Selections**, and so on.
- **Scripting Engine**: As QlikView can use VBScript and Jscript, establish one as a site standard as this would make maintenance easier.
- **Module Code**: Try to use only **Safe Mode** when writing **Module Code** as this makes the server implementation of the document easier and more secure.
- **Functions**: If you have functions stored in variables, keep a copy of the variable name and its contents stored in the script either as a `SET` function or as a commented section of code. Then, you'll have a working copy if someone changes the function. Note that if your function contains dollar sign expressions, don't store them as a `SET` statement since these will be expanded as part of script execution. You could also store functions and/or variables in a script file and simply include the script file in each application as a standard feature.
- **Script**: Break scripts into several separate tabs and avoid having excessively long sections of code on each tab.
- **Screen Size**: Establish what screen size should be used as a minimum and set this as your working canvas; the **View | Resize Window** option can help here.
- **Sheet Properties**: Always change all sheet properties to prevent users from moving objects around, and apply them to all sheets before you deploy your document to UAT or production.
- **Document Properties**: On the **Security** tab, always select **Admin Override Security**.

Hidden features – Easter eggs

As with many other products, QlikView has a hidden set of features, which are often referred to as Easter eggs.

Background

The Easter eggs in QlikView open up a number of settings that are not available elsewhere; although, you may recognize some that can also be set through the developer interface. There are over 400 settings available, and it is not advisable to change some of them. However, the three that we describe in detail here you may find useful.

How to do it

The Easter eggs are hidden away in the **Help** menu. Click on **About QlikView**, and a pop-up window will be displayed, showing you the version and license details. To the lower-left is the Qlik logo:

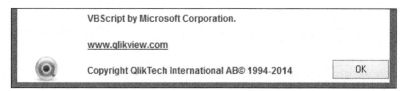

If you let the mouse hover over the logo and then right-click on it, the Easter egg window appears:

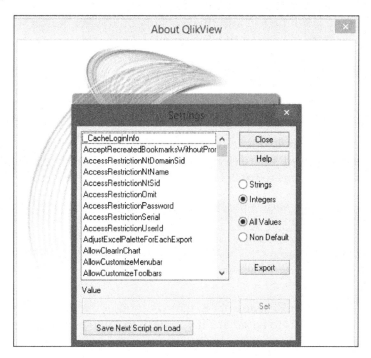

Here, you can make changes to many settings that are not available elsewhere.

The following screenshot shows the **AllowMacrosFunctionsInExpressions** attribute:

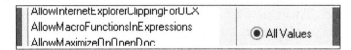

When you create a function with VBScript or JScript in the module editor, the functions are only available to your load script. However, setting the **AllowMacroFunctionsInExpressions** attribute to **1** allows the functions to be available to all expressions, including charts and graphs.

To do this, first click on **AllowMacroFunctionInExpressions** in the list, enter **1** in the value box at the bottom of the form, and then click on the **Set** button.

The following screenshot shows the **ApplicationRescue** attribute:

Another useful feature is the ability to open corrupt QVW files. Normally, QlikView does not open a file if it appears to be corrupt. However, setting the **ApplicationRescue** attribute to **1** and then clicking on the **Set** button will allow QlikView to at least try to recover the document.

> This may be something you leave until you have a corrupt document as at least having the error message first will warn you of the issue.

It may not recover the whole document, but in some cases, a little is better than none at all. If you have followed our advice in the previous chapter, you should have a couple of previous versions to try before resorting to this option.

The following screenshot shows the **ScriptRescue** attribute:

As well as the **ApplicationRescue** option, there is another that needs to be set. The **ScriptRescue** option needs to be set to **1** if you wish to try to recover the script as well.

Many of the settings available in the Easter eggs list are available via the developer interface, and we recommend that you change these using the appropriate screen options. However, we mentioned three here that we found useful when developing applications. We can't see why you would not want to have a VBScript or Jscript function available throughout an application. Likewise, on the rare occasion when a document does become corrupt, it's helpful to have at least some chance of recovering some or all of it.

A few do's and don'ts

There are some things you should always do, and some you just shouldn't! You will find many little things in QlikView that you need to lock away in your memory, and they'll all add to your overall skill level.

Background

Some do's and don'ts may be thought of as best practice or useful site standards, but here are a few that work better on a personal level.

How to do it

Do:

- **Use F1**: QlikView's syntax is different from other languages. Use the *F1* key to bring up context-sensitive help, showing you the full syntax and parameter list. This helps you learn the syntax and helps ensure that you get the correct results from the start.
- **Drop Table**: Drop Table in the script is a good way of making things more efficient. Remember, though, that dropping one table with identical fields to another will drop both!
- **Drop Fields**: If you drop fields, use a list rather than individual statements; it is much more efficient.
- **Use the fora**: Sometimes, QlikView throws up something odd that does not seem to have a solution and isn't in the manual. Check out the fora because there's a good chance that someone else would have had the same problem.
- **Read blogs**: There are quite a few regular QlikView bloggers, and quite often, there's a useful gem on a blog that saves hours of frustration in development.
- **Read books**: It might seem obvious, but reading a few books will fill in the gaps left by the manuals.

Don't:

- **Change Easter egg settings**: Never change an Easter egg setting you don't understand, unless you can restore the environment if everything goes wrong.
- **Forget security**: Always save a copy of your document and keep it safely before adding security (**Section Access**). Making a mistake in security can lock you out of your document, and there is no way back!
- **Remove All Values**: Don't use **File | Reduce Data | Remove All Values** if you have list boxes with **Always One Selected Value** as QlikView will unset the option on the next reload. As an alternative, select a single item (preferably the lowest level available, such as an invoice or a single employee); then, from the **Reduce Data** menu item, select **Keep Possible Values**. This will remove all unselected data from your document, leaving just what is selected and hopefully reducing the size of the QVW, while keeping the **Always Once Selected Value** property intact.
- **Give up**: At times, QlikView can be infuriating as code may not work the way you think it should. Remember that there are always several ways to do things in QlikView; so, if something doesn't seem to work, try a different approach!

Summary

In this chapter, we showed you numerous tips and tricks to make you more productive and ensure that you don't lose your work when things go wrong. Some of these ideas are best practices, while others are simply not documented at all. These are all the things you need to know to help take your skills to the next level.

4
It's All About Understanding the Data

In this chapter, we will cover the following key topics:

- Understanding the data you're working with
- Even a few list and table boxes tell you and the user a lot
- Exciting users with a prototype, then throwing it away
- Dirty data and what to do about it
- Is this the right place for this data?
- Building a structure of QVD layers
- Incremental loads and performance

Understanding the data you're working with

Having a general understanding of the data and where it comes from is of vital importance for any QlikView application.

Background

QlikView is nothing without data, and without at least a reasonable understanding of the data needed, you will be missing a vital part of the development process. The data may come from several sources, and an overall understanding of these sources is also important. However, detailed knowledge isn't required—just enough to know when something feels right or wrong. If you happen to have detailed knowledge of the source systems, that's good news, but don't get too hung up on trying to learn every detail as you'll never get to start work on your QlikView application.

How to do it

Most applications use more than one data source, whether it is two or more database tables or multiple tabs from a spreadsheet. While an understanding of the source of the data is important, it is far more important to understand the data itself. There are several aspects to this process.

The most important part of a QlikView application is the data model. It takes time and skill to build an effective and efficient data model. If the data model is well-designed, it tends to make the development of objects simpler and quicker. The key to a good data model is an understanding of the keys common to each incoming data source. Getting this right is vital. Don't be afraid to spend time on this; often, the design of the data model and the scripting necessary to build it can account for 50 to 60 percent of the total development of a complex application.

Take time to understand what data is needed and, just as importantly, what isn't needed. Don't load data that isn't needed. If you think it might be needed at some point, by all means include it in the script but comment it out. Don't forget to comment the script, stating why this has been done. (Use // to comment single lines or /* and */ to enclose blocks of code. Remember that you can select code in the editor by clicking and dragging and then right-clicking to get a pop-up menu that allows you to comment—or uncomment—the code).

Work out what needs to be done to make the data from different systems work. For example, are the names of columns identical? Is the format of the data the same in different systems, and are dates all in the same format? Is the data structure the same, or is some reformatting required? Is any data duplicated across systems, and does some of this duplication need to be removed?

Don't be afraid to spend time understanding the data you're working with.

It can help build a temporary application that pulls in the data, and this is usually time well spent. This can help to identify relationships, potential areas of difficulty, and poor quality data. Just as QlikView helps users identify trends and outliers, a temporary load of some or all source data helps you understand how the data fits (or doesn't fit) together. Use the very valuable lessons from this exercise to develop a script and data model.

Get the data model and the scripting for it right, and the rest of the application will be easier to build and will perform better. Spending time on this pays more dividends than any other aspect of QlikView development.

Even a few list and table boxes tell you and the user a lot

As we discussed in the previous section, understanding the data is a vital step in the development process. In this section, we will take a look at building a temporary application to assist this process.

Background

It is important for the developer to understand the data well enough to create a robust application, and building a temporary application for this is a useful step. However, the temporary application can have a second valuable use. Working with the user as the application is built usually generates many ideas from the user, and these can be incorporated into the final application. Sometimes, completely unexpected insights occur—but then, that's really what QlikView is all about. Use the time spent with the user to obtain a picture of the features and requirements of the final application.

It's All About Understanding the Data

How to do it

This exercise can take a few minutes or a couple of hours, but it's time well spent. The time required depends on how many data sources there are and the complexity of the data, but always start simply. You may not have access to all the data sources you require and be obliged to use extracts in spreadsheets or flat files when the real data is actually in a database. Load up just one or two tables or tabs to start with, and create some simple list boxes for known or suspected key fields. Create a table box for each incoming table or worksheet, and take a look at what results are shown when certain selections are made. This will help guide you as you gradually add in more data sources.

Review your findings with the user. If they are with you as you work through the loading process, it would help as they may recognize certain data and guide you quickly to conclusions that you might not easily reach on your own.

You will soon start to see data relationships, and possibly discover that required data is missing. This exercise would also reveal any poor quality data, and this may be the first sign that a data cleansing project is required.

> New QlikView developments very often become the catalyst for data cleansing projects, so don't be surprised.

In the following examples, we can see the relationship between `Customer`, `SalesOrderHeader`, and `SalesOrderLine`. However, as soon as the `Supplier` and `Product` tables are added, there is a data loop (sometimes called a **Circular Reference**). This is indicated in the table viewer with dashed lines between the tables. We'll look at how to deal with data loops in the next chapter, in the section, *Avoiding loops in the data model*.

Code to load `Customer`, `SalesOrderHeader`, and `SalesOrderLine` is shown in the following screenshot:

```
Main

 1  SET ThousandSep=',';
 2  SET DecimalSep='.';
 3  SET MoneyThousandSep=',';
 4  SET MoneyDecimalSep='.';
 5  SET MoneyFormat='£#,##0.00;-£#,##0.00';
 6  SET TimeFormat='hh:mm:ss';
 7  SET DateFormat='DD/MM/YYYY';
 8  SET TimestampFormat='DD/MM/YYYY hh:mm:ss[.fff]';
 9  SET MonthNames='Jan;Feb;Mar;Apr;May;Jun;Jul;Aug;Sep;Oct;Nov;Dec';
10  SET DayNames='Mon;Tue;Wed;Thu;Fri;Sat;Sun';
11
12
13  Customer:
14  LOAD [Customer No],
15       [Customer Name],
16       [Address Line 1],
17       [Address Line 2],
18       [Address Line 3]
19  FROM
20  [QlikView Unlocked Data Chapter 4.xlsx]
21  (ooxml, embedded labels, table is Customer);
22
23
24  SalesOrderHeader:
25  LOAD [Order No],
26       [Order Date],
27       Status,
28       [Customer No],
29       [Completed Date]
30  FROM
31  [QlikView Unlocked Data Chapter 4.xlsx]
32  (ooxml, embedded labels, table is [Sales Order Header]);
33
34
35  SalesOrderLine:
36  LOAD [Order No],
37       [Line No],
38       [Product Code],
39       [Quantity Ordered]
40  FROM
41  [QlikView Unlocked Data Chapter 4.xlsx]
42  (ooxml, embedded labels, table is [Sales Order Line]);
43
```

Here's the data model for the load script shown above:

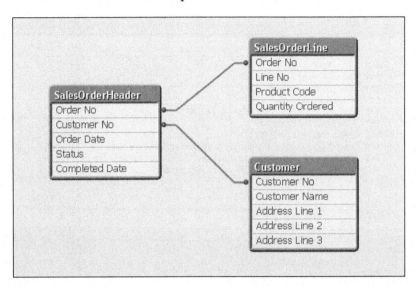

The following screenshot shows additional code to load `Supplier` and `Product`:

```
45  Supplier:
46  LOAD [Supplier No],
47       [Supplier Name],
48       [Address Line 1],
49       [Address Line 2],
50       [Address Line 3]
51  FROM
52  [QlikView Unlocked Data Chapter 4.xlsx]
53  (ooxml, embedded labels, table is Supplier);
54
55
56  Product:
57  LOAD [Product Code],
58       [Supplier Product Code],
59       [Supplier No],
60       [Manufacturer Product Code],
61       [Manufacturer No],
62       [Short Desciption],
63       Kit,
64       Price
65  FROM
66  [QlikView Unlocked Data Chapter 4.xlsx]
67  (ooxml, embedded labels, table is Product);
68
```

Finally, here's the data model after loading `Supplier` and `Product`:

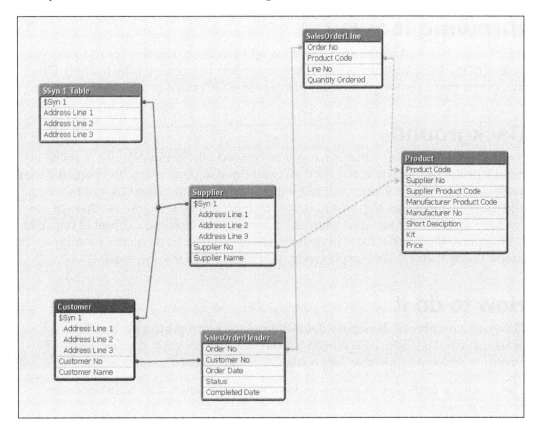

If you start your development with these simple steps and gradually build up an idea of how the data fits together, you'll be well on your way to building a great application. Always try to discuss this step with the user, preferably as you load the data into your temporary application. Don't try to do anything clever or visually stunning at this stage—this can come later. For now, just focus on understanding the data and capturing ideas from the user—as well as your own, of course!

Exciting users with a prototype, then throwing it away

As consumers, we all like to see what we might purchase, whether it's in a store or online. In the same way, users like to see something before they fully commit. Often, this means that a prototype or **proof of concept** (**POC**) must be built.

Background

It's hard to sell something that can't be seen or touched. Fortunately, it's possible to build a prototype quickly with QlikView, and this can be shown to the potential user audience. If you have already worked with the user to understand the data sources and likely features, this step would follow on quite easily. It is possible that you do not have access to the real data sources, and you could be using a subset of data that is in a spreadsheet or flat file. This is fine; however, never build on the prototype code—throw it away! We'll explain why you should take this approach.

How to do it

There are a number of dictionary definitions of the word **prototype**, but the one nearest to what needs to be achieved is from www.thefreedictionary.com: *"the original or model on which something is based or formed; pattern"*.

The prototype you create is a basis and not the end product. This is an important point to remember.

The prototype shows what can be done, so it includes some nice touches, such as an expression in a table object caption that shows how many rows are displayed. Another possibility is to conditionally display an object when certain selections are made. As a QlikView developer, you already know what can be done, right?

 The point of the prototype is more the presentation of possibilities rather than hard facts.

Don't spend lots of time ensuring that every object is complete or each calculation is 100 percent correct. Explain to the user audience that this is about the presentation, so put in some graphics and colorful charts.

It is almost certain that you will not have the real data sources available to you. Prototypes usually have to use spreadsheets as inputs, which normally means coding in the script to work around various problems or shortcomings. You may need to develop some QVDs for the real application, so it will probably not be available to use in the prototype. The point is that the prototype should be minimally engineered and built quickly. Ensure that users realize that it isn't necessarily real data that they are seeing.

Once the prototype has been demonstrated, use it for reference but not as the basis for code. Replicate parts of the data model that haven't changed but don't reuse the code—it probably refers to a spreadsheet, while the QVD that you really need may look different.

> Prototypes should be built fast but not to last. Use the ideas, not the code. Throw the prototype away when you've taken ideas from it.

The prototype is a starting point for what can or may be in the final application, but it's definitely not the end point. It should never be a fully working application and it doesn't have to behave perfectly or look completely finished. Just ensure that there's enough to interest the user and that you have the right audience. In other words, ensure that the real decision makers are involved when the prototype is demonstrated. Your own circumstances will dictate what features need to be included, whether it's special icons that are actually buttons, pictures, or maps. Your prototype is an indicator of the direction of travel, not the final destination. Save the rigorous development for the production version.

Dirty data and what to do about it

A major use of QlikView is to create Data Quality Dashboards as the issue of Data Quality affects everyone and is something that we need to bear in mind when designing the data model.

Background

Different data sources have their own levels of quality issues. Databases have field types, which, at least, prevent errors such as text in a numeric field or an invalid date entry in a date field. However, spreadsheets usually do very little in the way of verification. Always try to work with clean data, even if it means extra work before starting the real development work. Ideally, you can ask the data provider to clean up the data for you!

How to do it

Whatever our data source, we have to assume that there could be issues in the data because what works today may fail to refresh correctly tomorrow.

Data Quality can basically be broken down into three types:

- Incorrect or erroneous data
- Inconsistent data
- Duplication

To explain further, incorrect or erroneous data could be a date field typed as `10-May-2100` instead of `10-May-2010`, for example.

Inconsistent data, for instance, could be country types of `USA`, `U.S.A.`, or `United States`. All are valid, but if this field is used for selections, the user will not get a true picture. If it is used as a link between different sources, this would also cause problems.

Duplication may be an issue if the database is created from other sources and there is a chance that the same extract may be added twice. For example, an automatic upload fails and is manually triggered to refresh the document. Once the issue with automation is resolved, the automation part of the process can add the same data again.

There is no magical solution to all of these issues, and how they are handled in the data model depends on the type of data that is being loaded; however, hopefully, we can give you a few ideas. Think about the issue at design time. How incorrect data is handled is something that needs careful consideration—do you try to correct it or reject the record? Both can have a major effect on your document.

Incorrect or erroneous data

Spotting these errors may not be easy; a date of birth `10-May-1965` entered as `10-May-1956` would not be obvious unless we had a separate field with the age; although, age is usually calculated from the date of birth. However, if we had `Invoice Date` with the year `2105`, this would be easy to spot; in this case, we could have the following line in our load script:

```
If([Invoice Date]>Today(), Today() , [Invoice Date] ) as [Invoice Date],
```

Here, we checked the Invoice Date value against today's date. If the former is greater, we will use today's date; otherwise, the Invoice Date field's content will be used. This will work as long as we don't postdate our invoices; in this case, we could change >Today() to something similar to >Today()+31, which would add 31 days to today's date before replacing it.

 Use the Today() function rather than the Now() function, especially in object expressions, as the Now() function causes all expressions to be evaluated every second.

In some cases, a field might contain nulls. If this field is used for a calculation, the calculation would fail; so, use the ALT() function to change the nulls to another value (usually zero).

Inconsistent data

Where freehand entry is allowed in fields, the content's style is left to the user. They may enter everything in lowercase, uppercase, or capitalized. Users also may or may not add commas to the end of address lines, and country names may be written in many formats—for example, USA, U.S.A., or United States.

To help us with these, QlikView has a number of functions that will help us, which are shown in the following table:

Function	Use	Example
Capitalize	This converts a string so that the first letter of each word is in capitals and the rest is in lower case	Capitalize([Country]) as [Country] This will convert england to England
PurgeChar	This removes a character from a string	PurgeChar([Country],'.,;:') as [Country] This will remove punctuations from the field so that U.S.A becomes USA
Upper	This converts the whole string to uppercase	Upper([Country]) as [Country] This will convert a field to all uppercase so that England becomes ENGLAND
ApplyMap	This applies a mapping table to a field	Refer to the following section

The most useful of these statements is the `ApplyMap` function. To use it, you have to first load a mapping table as follows:

```
CountryMap:
Mapping LOAD * INLINE [
    From, To
    u.s.a, USA
    usa,   USA
    united states, USA
    united states of america, USA
    america, USA
    uk, United Kingdom
    u.k., United Kingdom

];
```

This script creates a mapping table with the inconsistent entries in the first column and the replacements in the second.

> A mapping table is the same as any other table except that field names are not used and the table is automatically dropped when the script finishes.

We would then use the following to do the conversion:

```
ApplyMap('CountryMap',Lower([Country])) as [Country]
```

We can combine all the options into a single statement with the following code:

```
ApplyMap('CountryMap',Lower([Country]),
Capitalize(PurgeChar([Country],',.;:' ))) as [Country]
```

Here the `Country` field is mapped against our table list; any country that is not in the list is then capitalized, having first removed all punctuation characters.

It is especially important to standardize a format style if this field is being used as a key field or as a user selection.

Duplication

There are two ways we can try to remove duplicate entries: one is with the DISTINCT option, and the other is with the EXISTS() function.

If our table has a unique identifier, which we can simply add to the end of our load statement:

```
Where not Exists([OrderNo])
```

This would only load records where the OrderNo (or other unique field) value is not in existence.

 If the unique field is a key field, ensure that this load is done before other tables that use the same key.

If we don't have a unique field to work with, our alternative is the DISTINCT option:

```
Load Distinct
```

Here, the DISTINCT option tells QlikView to only load records that don't already exist in the table. All fields are used for the comparison, and there is a performance hit as this is processor heavy.

Is this the right place for this data?

It can be tempting to try to build everything into one document to save on QlikView licenses. Here, we will explain why this is not a good strategy.

Background

There are often good reasons to want to cram as many features or disassociated data as possible into a single QlikView document, but this is rarely the best strategy and can ultimately lead to difficult and expensive rewrites. Keep logically different applications in separate documents and take the hit on QlikView license costs because, ultimately, this will be cheaper and save you lots of time.

How to do it

We can't always anticipate how a QlikView document will evolve, and even the best-designed application could eventually become unwieldy and inefficient over time. Often, this is caused by adding in data and features that would be better in a separate document. It's common to see QlikView documents that should logically be two or more documents, with unrelated data models or simply too many features, crammed into a single document in an effort to save on QlikView license costs.

 Don't be tempted to cram too much into one document. In the long run, chances are that you will end up rewriting the application or working through a very difficult reengineering job.

As an example of a document that should have been created as two documents, consider one with human resources data covering absenteeism and purchase orders. These are unrelated application areas, which almost certainly means that there should be two completely distinct data models within the application. This isn't good for performance; it is unwieldy and almost certainly difficult to maintain. It could also imply some unnecessarily tricky security issues. In this case, the document should have definitely been developed as two separate documents from the outset.

A different problem might be a document with billions of rows of general ledger data, which also holds a lot of detailed supplier data, including invoice details. While these two areas are logically connected, there could well be a performance issue. In addition, the supplier data and general ledger data may require different security arrangements. Ideally, the general ledger data would appear in one document and the supplier data in a separate document. The users of the general ledger document who are authorized to use the supplier document could launch the supplier document from an action (usually a button). Refer to the 'External' action type and 'Launch' action in QlikView Help for details. Remember that launching one document from another requires two User CALs!

Always think about who would use the document and what they would use it for because this will guide you to only pull in the data that is really needed. Don't pull in data that isn't used, because it wastes resources and adds no value at all. Also, look out for fields that add very little value and decide whether they are really necessary. For example, long unstructured texts, such as comment fields, rarely add value and use a lot of memory because their contents are unique and QlikView is not able to apply any compression to them.

Chapter 4

Building a structure of QVD layers

Designing and building ETL layers of QVDs can pay dividends as your use of QlikView grows.

Background

Always try to plan your use of database tables in advance. It's usually much better to start by devising your QVD layers from the outset than to create them later and then having to rework the applications you have already created. QVDs are extremely efficient; as soon as you have the requirement to read the same source data twice or more, one extraction to QVD and then reading (and if necessary, manipulating) a QVD multiple times is generally faster than reading the database table several times into each application that requires it.

How to do it

Consider these scenarios:

- **Scenario 1**: A QlikView application that reads six database tables and does some transformation on each of them
- **Scenario 2**: A QlikView application that reads six QVD files that require no transformation

If scenario 1 has a failure on the reading of the sixth table for some reason, it could be very time-consuming to rerun it because it will be necessary to read and transform the first five tables all over again. However, if the reading of the sixth QVD file fails in scenario 2, it would only be necessary to fix this QVD file before rerunning the application; as it reads QVD files, it would be much faster. Furthermore, as the QVD files require no transformation, the read would be optimized and run many times faster than an unoptimized read.

> Loading from a QVD file is much faster if you don't need to do any manipulation on it. This is called an **optimized load**, and it will still be optimized if you use a WHERE EXISTS clause or change a field name using a AS b. However, using a function on a field or any other variation of the WHERE clause would cause the load to be unoptimized.

[67]

You will no doubt be thinking: that's all very well, but you would need to prepare these QVD files; you're quite right. However, if these QVD files are used in other applications, they would have been created by only reading the database once, not by each application.

For these reasons, you should seriously consider a two-or three-layer approach to building applications. If yours is an extremely complex environment, you may need more layers.

In a single layer, the same database table may be read and transformed many times over by different applications.

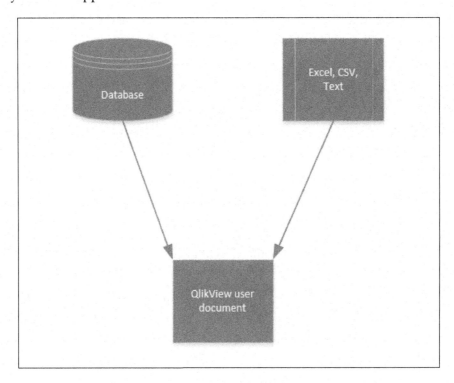

If the environment is a relatively simple one, it may only be necessary to have two layers. The first layer does the extracting and transforming, while the second is the GUI.

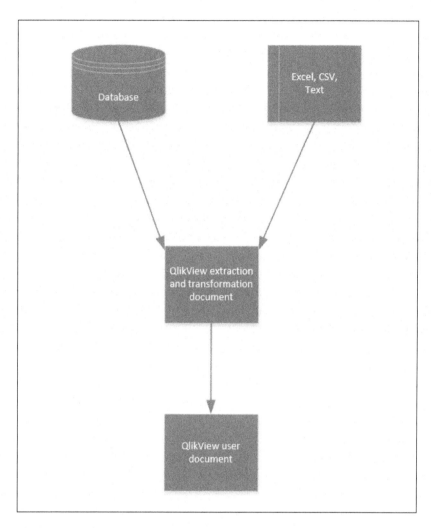

Most environments of any size benefit from a three-layer design. The first layer handles just the extraction, the second handles transformation, and the third is the GUI. The transformation layer allows a lot of flexibility to be introduced while using just one set of database extractions. Furthermore, you can save hours of processing because the extractions can be run in parallel. Bear in mind, though, that you will not be able to sequence tasks based on "on successful completion".

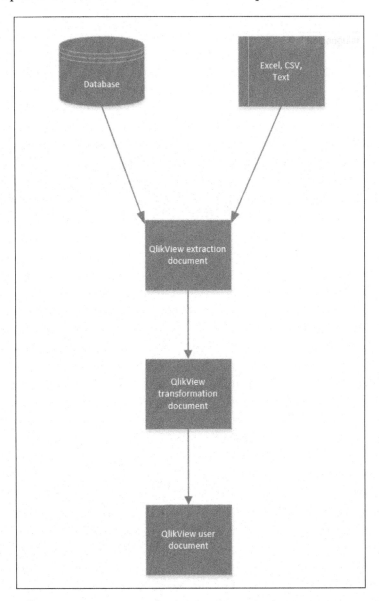

Incremental loads and performance

Most data sources grow over time, and when dealing with large volumes of data, the time taken to reload documents increases along with the size of the data.

Background

The time taken to read all the data from a file or database increases as the size of the data grows, especially if this source is on the wrong side of a firewall or on an older, slower network infrastructure.

One way to reduce the time taken for the reload is to only load from source data that has been added or changed, reducing the amount of data retrieved from the source.

The less data that needs to pulled from a database, spreadsheet, or text file, the quicker the reload will be. Reading the bulk of the data from a QVD file is substantially faster.

How to do it

Incremental load is a technique whereby data is read from a source and stored on a local drive as a QVD file. Subsequent loads are first done from the QVD file; then, only the new (or updated) data is read from the source and finally saved again as a replacement QVD file ready for the next time.

There are a couple of techniques that can be used to accomplish an incremental load, and which of these to use depends on a couple of factors you need to establish.

Firstly, establish where the data is coming from: is it a text file (such as a log file), a spreadsheet, or database table?

Secondly, is data just added to the source or is it updated? Or, are there records possibly deleted too?

The simplest form is when reading a text file (such as a system log), where data is only added to the end. For this, there is a simple prefix to the QlikView load instruction.

The following script will read the entire QlikView session log:

```
SessionLog:
LOAD *
FROM
[C:\ProgramData\QlikTech\QlikViewServer\Sessions_QLIKVIEW.log]
(txt, utf8, embedded labels, delimiter is '\t', msq);
```

Every time the document is reloaded, the entire file will be read; however, we could change it to the following:

```
SessionLog:
Buffer(Incremental)
LOAD *
FROM
[C:\ProgramData\QlikTech\QlikViewServer\Sessions_QLIKVIEW.log]
(txt, utf8, embedded labels, delimiter is '\t', msq);
```

You will notice the addition of a single line, `Buffer(Incremental)`, which tells QlikView to create its own temporary QVD file the first time the file is read and to remember the size of the source file. Next time, it will read the QVD file first and add to it anything from that saved point onwards before finally saving the revised QVD file and pointer.

This method works well and is easy to implement but can only be used for simple text files (including CSV) where data is only appended.

> Look at the QlikView help topic for other buffer options as there are quite a few useful variations of this prefix.

If data comes from a more complex source, such as a database table or spreadsheet, a different approach is needed. First of all, it is necessary to establish whether there is a field that can be used as a marker. Ideally, there is an autonumber record ID that is increased with every record, a timestamp field when the record is written (or updated), or a date field, such as `Order Created`. (Care must be taken here as performing multiple refreshes in one day could cause an issue with duplicates.)

If you cannot identify a suitable field, the incremental load approach is not possible.

In this example, it is necessary to write a lot more script to handle this approach as there needs to be resilience for times when a total refresh is required or for the first time the document is loaded.

Take a look at the following script:

```
If IsNull(FileTime('ShopSales.qvd')) then

  ShopSales:
  LOAD [Shop No],
       [Product Code],
       Quantity,
       [Sale Date]
  FROM [QlikView Unlocked Data Chapter 4.xlsx]
  (ooxml, embedded labels, table is [Shop Sale]);

ELSE
  ShopSales:
  LOAD * From 'ShopSales.qvd' (qvd);

  Temp:
  Load Max([Sale Date]) as MaxDate
  Resident ShopSales;

  LET varMaxDate=peek('MaxDate',0,'Temp');

  DROP Table Temp;

  Concatenate(ShopSales)
  LOAD [Shop No],
       [Product Code],
       Quantity,
       [Sale Date]
  FROM [QlikView Unlocked Data Chapter 4.xlsx]
  (ooxml, embedded labels, table is [Shop Sale])
    where [Sale Date]>'$(var MaxDate)';

ENDIF

Store ShopSales into ShopSales.qvd (qvd);
```

The first thing to do is to identify whether the holding QVD file exists. The first time this script is run, it won't exist, so a full load of the data is needed from the source. Also, if the integrity of the QVD file is questionable, it could be manually deleted and the whole file will be refreshed the next time the document is reloaded.

If the QVD file doesn't exist, the whole source file is read, as it would have happened without using incremental load.

The real incremental load is performed after the ELSE statement. QlikView will first read in the previous QVD file, and as there is no manipulation of data taking place, the optimized load process will be used.

Now, it is necessary to establish the current end point of the existing data. This uses the field identified earlier as a marker field; in this instance, let's use [Sale Date]. This is done by creating a temporary table with a single record of the maximum value of the fields. The content of this record is read and stored into a variable using the peek() function. The table can be dropped when finished.

Now, we are ready to read the source file again, but this time, we will add Concatenate() at the beginning and a WHERE clause at the end. Concatenate tells QlikView to add data to the existing table, and the WHERE clause specifies the new records.

> If the Concatenate prefix is not used, the table will normally be concatenated automatically as the fields are the same; however, use Concatenate for easier reading. Should any further fields be added, this would force the process.

Finally, store the table in a local QVD file ready for the next time.

So far, we looked at data sources where we added data, but often there are situations where a lot of data is modified or records are removed. This creates even more challenges for incremental loads as existing records in the QVD have to be changed or removed.

With the previous method, it was necessary to identify a marked field to do the load from, but now we need to be able to identify which fields have been changed too. The only really safe method here is to have a timestamp field of when the record was created or modified. This way, it is possible to identify the records that need to be added or changed effectively, and more importantly, reliably.

Although there may be more script and complexity involved in using the incremental load techniques, the time saved while reloading a document can be enormous, especially as the source data grows.

The main point to remember is that you must build into your script the possibility that the QVD file no longer exists, and you need to do a full load. This is essential for the times when you suspect the integrity of the QVD, when the QVD file is accidentally deleted, or there are major changes to the source table.

> Try to keep the reading of the source as simple as possible. If there is any manipulation needed to be done on the records as they are read in, it is more efficient to do this as part of the incremental load process as it will only be done once and not every time the source is read.

Rather than reinvent the wheel, there is an excellent document on the Qlik website that describes the process and has example scripts for you to use. Have a look at the document at https://community.qlik.com/docs/DOC-4597

> Pay particular attention to the PowerPoint slides.

Performance

There are other ways to speed up the load script, but sometimes, you have to think outside of the box. As every server is different, there is no single easy answer to improving performance. Processor speed, memory capacity, disk configuration, and network speed all have an important role to play. It is worth trying different approaches on your system to find what works best.

Once you have loaded a table into memory, should you need to use it again, say, as part of an ETL process, it is assumed that the use of the Resident option would be the logical choice.

However, if the source of this table is a QVD file stored on a fast local drive, it can be a lot faster reading it again from the QVD file. This may have something to do with buffering, but we have found that, in many instances, it is worth trying.

If creating another copy of a table, again as part of the ETL process, you would normally create a new table using the Resident option and drop the original table when finished. However, if the table is large and there's not enough free RAM in the server, it will start paging and performance will rapidly deteriorate. An alternative is to use Store to store the table into a temporary QVD file, use Drop to drop the table, and then read the temporary QVD file from disk. This way, only one table is in memory at a time, and the time taken to save the table to disk can easily outweigh the time spent paging.

These are just a few ways to increase performance; you will have to try different approaches. Don't be afraid to try an alternative you don't believe will work; sometimes you will be surprised—we have been.

To help you with working out the most efficient approach, you might want to consider adding the following three lines to your script.

Put this line at the start of the script:

```
LET varTimer=Now();
```

Put these two lines at the end of the script (before any `EXIT SCRIPT` statement!):

```
LET varTimer=Time(Now()-varTimer);
TRACE Taken $(varTimer) to run;
```

This will show how long the script has taken to run on the refresh panel, the log file, and also stored as a variable. This should help to make it easier to time results.

> Remember to try different approaches a couple of times to get an average reading, as other server activity can affect your timings. Ideally, try to run the test when no other activity is taking place on the server.

Summary

In this chapter, we considered how to start building a prototype application, looking at what to do about dirty data, with some solutions to this very common problem. Then, we discussed QVD layers, incremental loads, and performance considerations.

5
The Right Data Model Pays Dividends

In this chapter, we will cover the following key topics:

- Synthetic keys and why they're sometimes bad news
- Link tables
- Avoiding loops in the data model
- Simplify, simplify, simplify – never have subtables that you don't need
- Data islands, single calendars, and set analysis
- Avoiding problems with JOIN

Synthetic keys and why they're sometimes bad news

Whenever you create two or more tables that have two or more fields with the same name, QlikView creates a synthetic key table to join them.

Background

Old school logic has stated for a long time that Synthetic keys in the data model design are bad. This is not always the case, however, and in some cases, it is unavoidable.

How to do it

The best way to avoid Synthetic keys is to create a single field with all the fields concatenated together. This needs to be done in all linking tables. The result would be a cleaner and potentially more efficient design.

The problem with this approach is the amount of memory it can consume. The uniqueness of this new combined field means that the amount of memory used to store it is increased and not just in one table but all of them, as in the following simple example.

Current fields:

Field	Number of unique entries	Bytes used
Invoice Date	50	500 (10 characters x 50)
Customer ID	100	800 (8 characters x 100)

With combined fields:

Field	Number of unique entries	Bytes used
Invoice Date	50	500 (10 characters x 50)
Customer ID	100	800 (8 characters x 100)
Invoice Date and Customer ID	2000 (not all combinations used)	36,000 (18 characters x 2000)

As you can see, there is a dramatic increase in memory requirement, and this will be duplicated at least twice (once for each table being linked); the preceding example only uses a small number of entities.

Leaving the synthetic key would result in an additional table with one set of the current fields; however, as you can see from the preceding figures, it does not consume anywhere near as much memory.

You could use the AUTONUMBER function to cut down the memory overhead of the extra field, but this will still take up space in the file's record pointer table, so it still has an impact on your memory usage.

> AUTONUMBER as a function is time consuming to execute; AUTONUMBERHASH128 and AUTONUMBERHASH256 are quicker, but do not support the multiple key option.
>
> If you use the INTERVALMATCH function in your script to create a bucket container, it will always generate a Synthetic key, and there is no way around this.

If you have the situation where the script appears to hang at the end of a data load, this is usually where QlikView is trying to resolve its synthetic keys. If you are not expecting synthetic keys to be generated, there could be an issue with your script that is generating them. Until the process is complete, you will not know where the issue is, and if the problem has resulted in a large table with many linked fields, this can take a very long time (sometimes many hours).

In this case, you may want to kill the task and reload under the debug option with only a limited record set. This is achieved by clicking on the **Debug** option in the script editor:

Then, tick the **Limit Load** option and if required, change the number of rows to read from each table from **10** to whatever you desire. However, remember that the more records read, the more synthetic keys will be created, so we recommend leaving it at **10**.

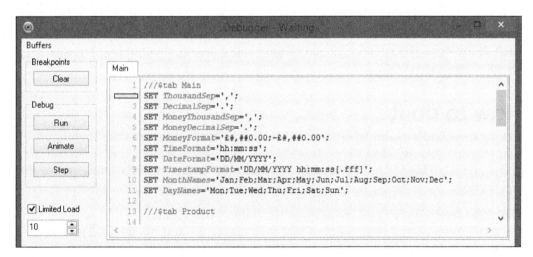

Click on the **Run** button to run the script, and this will reload the script with only **10** rows for each table. When the processing gets to the end of the script, it will only generate a synthetic key on a small table, which should be fairly quick. When it's finally finished, you can select the table view (**Internal View** rather than **Source View**) and see why the synthetic keys have been created.

The Right Data Model Pays Dividends

Although it is better to not have synthetic keys, it is too expensive, sometimes, on memory to avoid them. There would be a slight performance hit, as the additional table would be referenced during lookups. Everything still comes around to the long standing computing term of "Time/Space Compromise". For those who have not come across it, it states that getting the quickest results needs the most memory, and the things that use the least memory take the longest to process.

Have a look at the Qlik community forum item at `https://community.qlik.com/thread/10279`, which has a good discussion on this subject.

The jury is still out on whether synthetic keys are a bad thing or not, but for the most efficient performance they should be avoided.

Link tables

There are times when it is necessary to have two or more fact tables that have some common dimensions, but they are too big or complex to merge or join in a simple way.

Background

Let's take a typical example of a daily transaction table and a monthly budget/forecast table. They could have common fields that need to be shared as dimensions, such as the `Period`, `Product Type`, or `Region`, but having them in two separate tables would not work.

How to do it

Taking this simple example, we want to be able to connect these tables together so that we can not only select `Periods`, `Product Type` and/or `Region` (`Product Type` and `Region` are held in both tables) but also be able to find the forecast figure for the transactions.

Using the following script to read these two tables, you will notice that both alias the `Product Type` and `Region` fields so that they don't join, and the script also adds a unique ID field based on the record number (the Date field name is already different in both tables, so there's no need to alias that):

```
Transactions:
LOAD [Order Date],
     [Order No],
     [Product Code],
     [Product Type] as [Trans_Product Type],
     Supplier,
```

```
        Region as Trans_Region,
        Qty,
        Price,
        Total,
        RecNo() as Trans_ID
FROM Sales.xlsx
(ooxml, embedded labels, table is Daily);

Forecast:
LOAD [Month End],
     [Product Type] as [Forecast_Product Type],
     Region as Forecast_Region,
     Forecast,
     Manager,
     RecNo() as Forecast_ID
FROM Sales.xlsx
(ooxml, embedded labels, table is Forecast);
```

Once this script is executed, it results in these two tables:

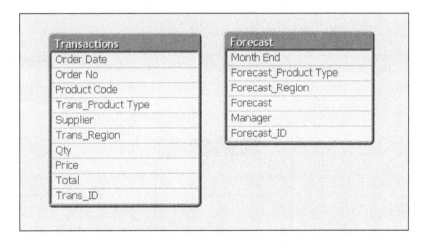

Note that there are no joins. This is where the Link table makes its appearance, so take a look at the following script.

```
Link_Table:
Load
  [Order Date]          as Link_Date,
  Year([Order Date])    as Link_Year,
  [Trans_Product Type]  as [Link_Product Type],
  Trans_Region          as Link_Region,
  Trans_ID
```

The Right Data Model Pays Dividends

```
Resident Transactions;

Concatenate(Link_Table)
Load
   [Month End]          as Link_Date,
   Year([Month End])    as Link_Year,
   [Forecast_Product Type] as [Link_Product Type],
   Forecast_Region      as Link_Region,
   Forecast_ID
Resident Forecast;
```

Here, we took the `Transaction` table and created a new table, aliasing all fields except `Trans_ID` (which we created earlier as a unique record identifier). We also created a Year field for selection purposes. (We could create additional items too if we want, such as Quarter.)

When the `Transactions` table has been read, we will add the `Forecast` table to the bottom of the new link table. Aliasing, once more, all the common fields except `Forecast_ID`; here again, we need to keep it separate.

We would now have the following data model:

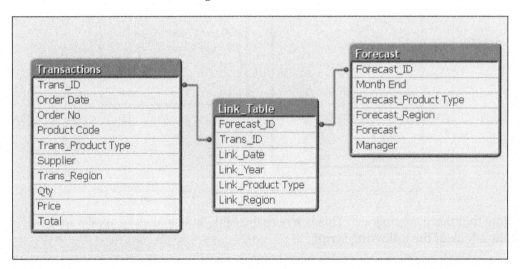

As you can see, the two original tables are now joined into to a single Link table.

Now, using the Link_Table fields as dimensions and selections, we can access the `Transactions` and `Forecast` data together.

As the original dimension fields are now surplus compared to our requirements, they could be removed to help reduce the memory overhead (unless, of course, they are specifically needed elsewhere). By adding these two lines, we can make the model even more efficient:

```
DROP Fields [Trans_Product Type], Trans_Region ;
DROP Fields [Forecast_Product Type], Forecast_Region ;
```

This technique can be used for as many fact tables as needed; just remember to create a separate unique key for each table.

In this example, we used the record number as the unique key, but if your data already has one, you should use it. Also, you may need to create a key as a combination of the existing fields.

> If you create a unique key by combining the existing fields, you may want to consider using the `Autonumber` function, which is described in the next chapter.

Avoiding loops in the data model

Loops—or as Qlik calls them, circular references—are to be avoided at all costs as far as QlikView is concerned.

Background

When creating a data model, it can be very easy to create circular references as you add in all your tables. As QlikView cannot handle these in its selection engine, they must be avoided. However, should your data model have them, QlikView "loosely couples" some of the offending tables. This means that the loosely coupled tables will not be restricted in any selection.

How to do it

Sometimes, having performed a reload of your data, you would get the following message:

The Right Data Model Pays Dividends

This indicates that QlikView has detected a circular reference and has loosely coupled some tables in the data model.

If you view your table structure (*Ctrl+T*), you will notice that there are some dashed lines connecting at least one table; this is where the circular reference has been detected and needs your attention.

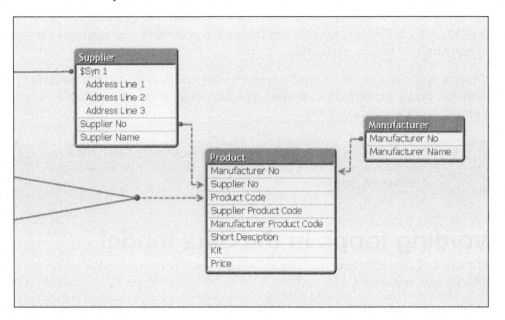

In many cases, including the preceding one, circular references are caused by commonly named fields being linked together (with synthetic keys or without) when they shouldn't be. Removing the synthetic keys or stopping the commonly named fields from linking by using aliases may solve the issue.

However, if you are still left with circular references after removing any erroneous links, you will need to look closely at the rest of your data model to find where you need to alias fields to break the circle.

If you leave them in place, any table affected by the loop will be loosely coupled, which will dramatically affect the document's ability to perform as you would like. In fact, it may not perform at all, as big portions of data may not be selected as expected.

Simplify, simplify, simplify – never have subtables that you don't need

Does good database design give the best results in QlikView?

Background

QlikView's data model design philosophy doesn't follow that of good database design; in fact, to get the best out of QlikView it is nearly the exact opposite.

For anyone who has been involved with database design, for many years the philosophy has been to have a fully normalized data structure. For those who don't know what this means, in simplistic terms, don't store anything twice. So, if you have, for example, a `Manufacturer Name` in each `Product` record, you should create a separate table to hold all the `Manufacturer Names` and a `Key` and then just store the appropriate `Key` in each of the `Product` records.

The `Manufacturer Name` will only be stored once in the database, taking up less space.

How to do it

QlikView quite happily works with a fully normalized database. However, from a QlikView perspective, the most efficient data model is one flat file with everything in it. Of course, this would mean that the `Manufacturer Name` will be repeated many times. This is where QlikView scores over other systems, as it is excellent at memory management and would only store one instance of a `Manufacturer Name` in memory.

As an example, look at the following script:

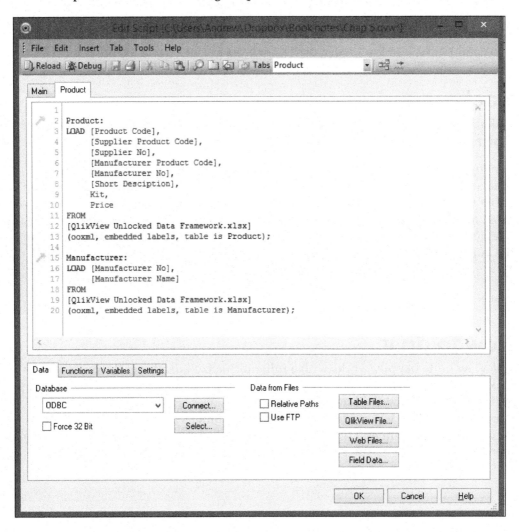

This generates two tables, similar to this:

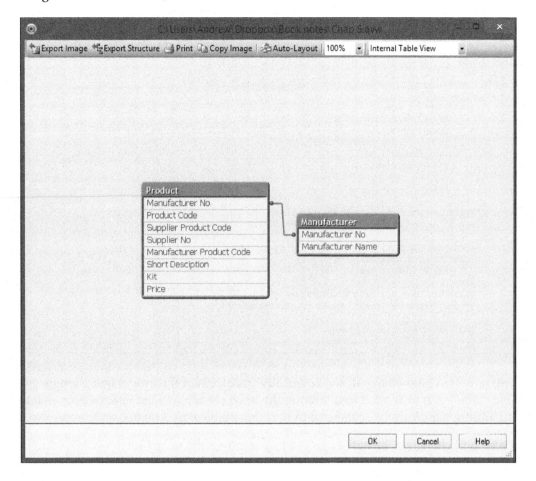

This works perfectly, but it's not the most efficient option for QlikView. With a bit of reworking, we can change this to a single table, which QlikView would be happier with. Consider the following:

```
Product:
LOAD [Product Code],
     [Supplier Product Code],
     [Supplier No],
     [Manufacturer Product Code],
     [Manufacturer No],
     [Short Desciption],
     Kit,
     Price
FROM
[QlikView Unlocked Data Framework.xlsx]
(ooxml, embedded labels, table is Product);

left join(Product)
LOAD [Manufacturer No],
     [Manufacturer Name]
FROM
[QlikView Unlocked Data Framework.xlsx]
(ooxml, embedded labels, table is Manufacturer);

DROP Field [Manufacturer No];
```

With only two lines changed, we drastically transformed the model into a single table. `Line 15` is now a left join, linking the `Product` table to the `Manufacturer` table and adding `Manufacturer Name` to the `Product` table based on `Manufacturer No`.

The second change is the new `Line 22` that removes the `Manufacturer No` field, which is no longer needed:

Although QlikView works with a Star or Snow Flake design model, the most efficient is a single flat table. However, this is rarely the model you end up with, so just remember that the flatter the better as far as QlikView is concerned. Be careful, though; sometimes, if this is taken to extremes, duplicate data or other undesired effects may arise.

Data islands, single calendars, and set analysis

Quite often within QlikView applications, it is necessary to use the same selection criteria over a number of fields. For example, you may want to have a date selection, which selects `Date Ordered` on one chart and `Date Received` on another chart.

Background

Previously, we mentioned circular references. One way in which these are created is when there is a `Date` selection in multiple date fields. The multiple dates exist so that we can produce charts, for example, using `Date Ordered` on one chart and `Date Received` on another.

We could avoid the circular reference by having two selection boxes, but we could then have the issue that only selected records fit with both selections.

The alterative to this is to use the Data Island approach.

The Right Data Model Pays Dividends

How to do it

The way around this is to have a Data Island, where a table is created with no connections to any other table. Have a look at the following script:

```
Temp:
Load
    Min([Date Ordered]) as MinDate,
    Max([Date Ordered]) as MaxDate
Resident OrderData;

let varMinDate=peek('MinDate',0);
let varMaxDate=peek('MaxDate',0);
DROP Table Temp;

Temp:
Load
    Min([Date Received]) as MinDate,
    Max([Date Received]) as MaxDate
Resident OrderData;

let varMinDate=if(peek('MinDate',0)<$(varMinDate), peek('MinDate',0) , $(varMinDate) ) ;
let varMaxDate=if(peek('MaxDate',0)>$(varMaxDate), peek('MaxDate',0) , $(varMaxDate) ) ;
DROP Table Temp;

TempCalendar:
LOAD
    $(varMinDate) + IterNo() - 1 AS Num,
    Date($(varMinDate) + IterNo() - 1) AS TempDate
AUTOGENERATE 1
WHILE $(varMinDate) + IterNo() - 1 <= $(varMaxDate);

MasterCalendar:
LOAD TempDate as [Selected Date],
    Year(TempDate) AS [Selected Year],
    Month(TempDate) AS [Selected Month],
    text(date(TempDate,'MMM yyyy')) as [Selected MonthYear]
RESIDENT TempCalendar
ORDER BY TempDate ASC;

DROP TABLE TempCalendar;
```

Here, we created a `MasterCalendar` table using the earliest and latest date in either the `Date Ordered` or `Date Received` field. The result is something similar to this:

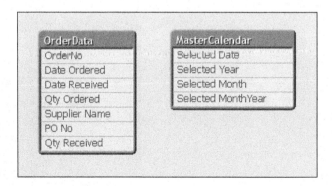

Note that the two tables are not linked in any way.

 You can add extra fields to the MasterCalendar table to give you extra selection criteria, such as Quarter, Week Number, and so on, so that these can be used in your selections.

Making a selection in any of the date fields will have no effect on the objects in the application here due to the fact that there is no link. What is now required is to add some Set Analysis code to the expression to activate the selections. To make this easier, create a variable in the script that contains the current active date range:

```
Set varSelectedDates= ='>=' & Min([Selected Date]) & '<=' & Max([Selected Date]);
```

This will now give you a variable with the earliest and latest dates within the current selection. If there is no selection, it will give the date range of the entire MasterCalendar. The dates are prefixed by the >= and <= range selectors so that they apply a selection within this range.

Now that we have everything in place, you can now add Set Analysis to the expression. If you needed to show the total of all Order Quantity each month, you would have needed an expression, such as the following:

```
Sum([ Qty Ordered ])
```

Here, you need the following:

```
Sum({$<[Date Ordered]={'$(varSelectedDates)'}>} [Qty Ordered])
```

By adding Set Analysis to the Date Ordered field, all reported records will now be within the selected range.

You could have another chart with the following expression:

```
Sum({$<[Date Received ] ={'$(varSelectedDates)'}>} [Qty Received])
```

This would apply the currently selected date range to the Date Received field rather than the Date Ordered field.

We showed you how to set up and use a Data Island with a date selection, but this can be used for any field that needs to be used in multiple cases.

Here are a few points to consider, though.

Firstly, every expression you have needs to have Set Analysis added to it, so table objects should not be used (because they don't support expressions).

Secondly, there will be a performance hit as every chart would have to calculate the Set Analysis selection, but as QlikView caches the calculations, this should be marginal (refer to *Cached Expressions* in *Chapter 7, Improving Chart Performance and Usability* for tips on caching).

Avoiding problems with JOIN

When using the JOIN function within QlikView, there are a few things to remember; otherwise, things can go disastrously wrong. However, it is the best way of cutting down the number of branches in a star data model.

Background

QlikView has four joining types; they are the same as SQL but there are slight differences in the syntax. QlikView uses `Inner`, `Outer`, `Left`, and `Right`, whereas SQL uses `Inner`, `Full`, `Left`, and `Right`. Using the right one with the right keys is essential.

How to do it

The easiest way to flatten the data model is to join two tables together into one. For a table where there is a key field and a description, it is very easy to add the description into the main table using a `LEFT` join (refer to the following section for an example.)

Data is joined using all the matching fields in the `Load` statement, so care must be taken to ensure that all fields needed are actually in the `Load` statement and that any field that is not needed as a link is aliased.

A further consideration is that if there are any duplicate records in the joining table, this will create duplicates in the receiving table too. One way to monitor this is to add the following two lines of code to the script, both before and after the join statement. This way, the log file will show if the main table has an increased number of rows when it shouldn't:

```
let varNoRows=NoOfRows('Product');
TRACE $(varNoRows);
```

Here, 'Product' is replaced with the name of the table being joined.

Care must also be taken to avoid a cartesian join as the resulting table could stop the script from running or cause it to take many hours to complete. If this happens, try refreshing using the debug option with the rows limited to 10 or 100. This way, you will be able to see if there is a large increase in rows, especially if you added the preceding two lines of script.

 A cartesian join is a join of every row of one table to every row of another table. This normally happens when no matching join fields are specified. For example, if table A with 250 rows is joined with table B with 2000 rows, a cartesian join will return 500,000 rows.

Here is an example:

```
Product:
LOAD [Product Code],
     [Supplier Product Code],
     [Supplier No],
     [Manufacturer Product Code],
     [Manufacturer No],
     [Short Desciption],
     Kit,
     Price
FROM
[QlikView Unlocked Data Framework.xlsx]
(ooxml, embedded labels, table is Product);

LET varNoRows=NoOfRows('Product');
TRACE $(varNoRows);


Left Join(Product)
LOAD [Manufacturer No],
     [Manufacturer Name]
FROM
[QlikView Unlocked Data Framework.xlsx]
(ooxml, embedded labels, table is Manufacturer);

DROP Field [Manufacturer No];

LET varNoRows=NoOfRows('Product');
TRACE $(varNoRows);
```

In this example script, there is a `Product` table which has a `Manufacturer No` field but no `Manufacturer Name` as this is held in a separate table. To make the data model more efficient, we can add `Manufacturer Name` to our `Product` table using a `Left` join.

Only records that are in the `Manufacturer` table with a matching `Manufacturer No` to that of the `Product` table will be added.

If there are any `Manufacturer No` fields that are not in the `Manufacturer` table, `Manufacturer Name` will contain a null.

As in the example, once the join is compete, we can remove the `Manufacturer No` field (unless we actually want to report on this as well) as most of the time, the linking field is just a pointer.

If you are planning a `Left` join with one or two fields with a single joining key, you may want to consider using a mapping table rather than a join. This can be more efficient and also offer you the option of setting the field value if there is no join field.

The preceding example could be rescripted to the following:

```
ManufName:
Mapping
LOAD [Manufacturer No],
     [Manufacturer Name]
FROM
[QlikView Unlocked Data Framework.xlsx]
(ooxml, embedded labels, table is Manufacturer);


Product:
LOAD [Product Code],
     [Supplier Product Code],
     [Supplier No],
     [Manufacturer Product Code],
     ApplyMap('ManufName',[Manufacturer No],'Missing')
         as [Manufacturer Name],
     [Short Description],
     Kit,
     Price
FROM
[QlikView Unlocked Data Framework.xlsx]
(ooxml, embedded labels, table is Product);
```

Here, we will first create a `Mapping` table to hold what was the `Left` join in our previous example. Then, we will load the main data from the `Product` table. We will use the `ApplyMap()` function to get the `Manufacturer Name` field and supply a piece of text when there is nothing to map.

As we do not need to store the `Manufacturer No` field, we do not need the `Drop` field statement either.

Depending on your server and data sources, this method can be more efficient than a `Left` join, so it is worth considering.

The following table gives a summary of join types:

Join type	Usage
Left	`Left Join (Table_A) * Resident Table_B`
	Fields from `Table_B` will be added to `Table_A` where there is a matching record in `Table_A` and `Table_B`.
Right	`Right Join (Table_A) * Resident Table_B`
	`Table_A` will now only contain records that exist in `Table_B` with the fields added from `Table_B`.
Inner	`Inner Join (Table_A) * Resident Table_B`
	`Table_A` will only contain records that are present in `Table_B`.
Outer	`Outer Join (Table_A) * Resident Table_B`
	`Table_A` will contain all records in `Table_A` or `Table_B`.

When things go wrong with a join, they tend to go very wrong!

If you have a cartesian join when you are not expecting it, your system could grind to a halt. The easiest way to resolve this, should it happen, is to refresh in **Debug** mode, with the **Limited Load** option ticked and set to 10. Then, look in the **Table View** screen and let the mouse hover over a table to ensure that the number of rows is correct.

For those of you that are familiar with SQL, there should be no issue with joins. However for the rest of you, don't be put off while using them to get the data model working well. After a while, it will be second nature.

Summary

In this chapter, we looked in great detail at how to build the data model, highlighting common problems and how to avoid them.

6
Make It Easy on Yourself – Some QlikView Tips and Tricks

In this chapter, we will cover the following key topics:

- A few coding tips
- Surprising data sources
- Include files
- Change logs
- Calculations and flags in the script
- `Previous()` and `Peek()` functions
- Preceding load on preceding load
- Finding min and max
- Autonumber
- Reading from a spreadsheet

A few coding tips

There are many ways to improve things in QlikView. Some are techniques, and some are just useful things to know or do. Here are a few of our favorite ones.

Keep the coding style constant

As you'll see in *Chapter 7, Improving Chart Performance and Usability*, there's actually more to this than just being a tidy developer. So, always code your function names in the same way—it doesn't matter which style you use (unless you have installation standards that require a particular style). For example, you could use `MonthStart()`, `monthstart()`, or `MONTHSTART()`. They're all equally valid, but for consistency, choose one and stick to it.

Use MUST_INCLUDE rather than INCLUDE

This feature wasn't documented at all until quite a late service release of v11.2, but it's very useful. If you use `INCLUDE` and the file you're trying to include can't be found, QlikView will silently ignore it. The consequences of this are unpredictable, ranging from strange behavior to an outright script failure. If you use `MUST_INCLUDE`, QlikView will complain that the include file is missing, and you can fix the problem before it causes you other issues. Actually, it seems strange that `INCLUDE` doesn't do this, but Qlik must have its reasons. Nevertheless, always use `MUST_INCLUDE` to save yourself time and effort.

Put version numbers in your code

QlikView doesn't have a versioning system as such, and we have yet to see one that works effectively with it. So, this requires some effort on the part of the developer. Devise a versioning system and always place the version number in a variable that is displayed somewhere in the application. It is not a matter of updating this number every time you make a change, but ensure that it's updated for every release to the user and ties in with your own release logs.

Do stringing in the script, not in screen objects

We would have put this in anyway, but its placement in the book was assured by a recent experience on a user site. They wanted four lines of address and a postcode strung together in a single field, with each part separated by a comma and a space. However, any field could contain nulls; so, to avoid addresses such as ",,,," or ", Somewhere,,,", there had be a check for null in every field as the fields were strung together. The table only contained about 350 rows, but it took 56 seconds to refresh on screen when the work was done in an expression in a straight table. Moving the expression to the script and presenting just the resulting single field on screen took only 0.14 seconds on screen. (That's right, about a seventh of a second.) Plus, it didn't adversely affect script performance. We can't think of a better example of improving screen performance.

Surprising data sources

QlikView reads database tables, spreadsheets, XML files, and text files, but did you know that it can also take data from a web page? If you need some standard data from the Internet, there's no need to create your own version. Just grab it from a web page! How about ISO Country Codes? Here's an example.

Open the script and click on **Web files...** below **Data from Files** on the right-hand side of the bottom section of the screen. This will open the **File Wizard: Source** dialogue.

Enter the URL where the table of data resides:

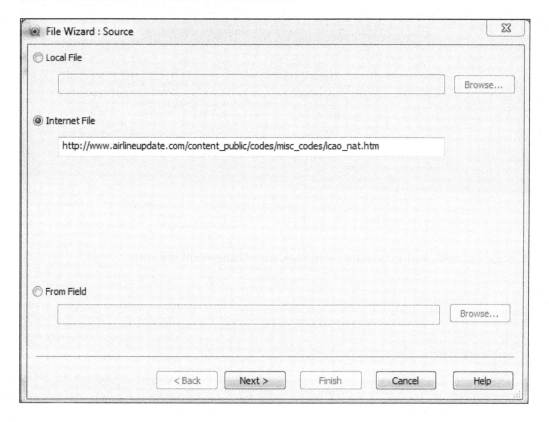

Then, click on **Next**; in this case, choose **@2** under **Tables**:

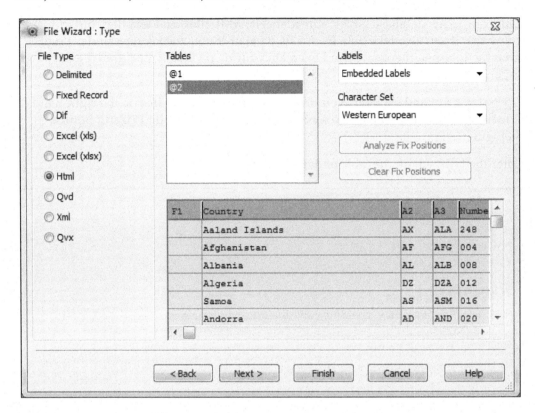

Click on **Finish**, and your script will look something similar to this:

```
LOAD F1,
     Country,
     A2,
     A3,
     Number
FROM
[http://www.airlineupdate.com/content_public/codes/misc_codes/icao_
nat.htm]
(html, codepage is 1252, embedded labels, table is @2);
```

Now, you've got a great lookup table in about 30 seconds—and another few seconds to clean it up for your own purposes. One small caveat though: web pages can change address, content, and structure, so it's worth putting in some validation around this if you think there could be any volatility.

Include files

We have already said that you should use MUST_INCLUDE rather than INCLUDE, but we're always surprised that many developers never use include files at all. If the same code needs to be used in more than one place, it really should be in an include file.

Suppose that you have several documents that use `C:\QlikFiles\Finance\Budgets.xlsx` and that the folder name is hardcoded in all of them. As soon as the file is moved to another location, you have several modifications to make, and it's easy to miss changing a document because you may not even realize it uses the file.

The solution is simple, very effective, and guaranteed to save you many reload failures.

Instead of coding the full folder name, create something similar to this:

```
LET vBudgetFolder='C:\QlikFiles\Finance\';
```

Put the line into an include file—for instance, `FolderNames.inc`.

Then, code this into each script:

```
$(MUST_INCLUDE=FolderNames.inc)
```

Finally, when you want to refer to your `Budgets.xlsx` spreadsheet, code the following:

```
$(vBudgetFolder)Budgets.xlsx
```

Now, if the folder path has to change, you only need to change one line of code in the include file, and everything will work fine as long as you implement include files in all your documents.

Note that this will work just as well for folders containing QVD files and so on. You can also use this technique to include LOAD from QVD files or spreadsheets because you should always aim to have just one version of the truth.

Change logs

Unfortunately, one of the things QlikView is not great at is version control. It can be really hard to see what has been done between versions of a document, and using the `-prj` folder feature can be extremely tedious and not necessarily helpful. So, this means that you, as the developer, need to maintain some discipline over version control.

To do this, ensure that right at the top of your script, you have an area of comments that looks something similar to this:

```
// Demo.qvw
//
// Roger Stone - One QV Ltd - 04-Jul-2015
//
// PURPOSE
// Sample code for QlikView Unlocked - Chapter 6
//
// CHANGE LOG
// Initial version 0.1
// - Pull in ISO table from Internet and local Excel data
//
// Version 0.2
// Remove unused fields and rename incoming ISO table fields to
// match local spreadsheet
//
```

Ensure that you update this every time you make a change. You could make this even more helpful by explaining why the change was made and not just what change was made. You should also comment expressions in charts when they are changed.

Chapter 6

Calculations and flags in the script

It's always a good idea to do as much work in the script as possible because the work only needs to be done once when the document is reloaded, not every time the user chooses a particular sheet or object.

Consider this requirement: products with prices between £10.00 and £19.99 need to be shown in a straight table with no other products visible. It would be easy enough to do this as an IF() statement in an expression:

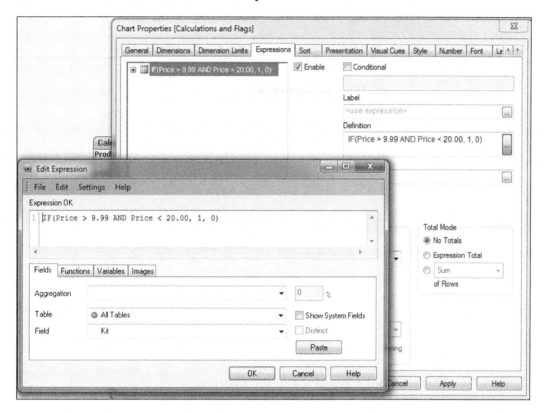

[103]

We suppress zero values and hide the column. However, if there are several thousand rows, screen performance could be poor.

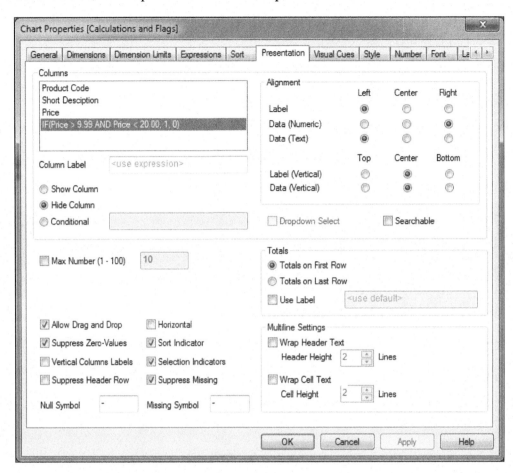

It would be better to do the work in the script if we can:

```
Product:
LOAD [Product Code],
     [Supplier Product Code],
     [Supplier No],
     [Manufacturer Product Code],
```

```
        [Manufacturer No],
        [Short Description],
        Kit,
        Price,
        IF(Price > 9.99 AND Price < 20.00, 1, 0) AS [Check Price]
FROM
[..\QlikView Unlocked Data.xlsx]
(ooxml, embedded labels, table is Product);
```

All we need to do now is have the new **[Check Price]** field as an expression:

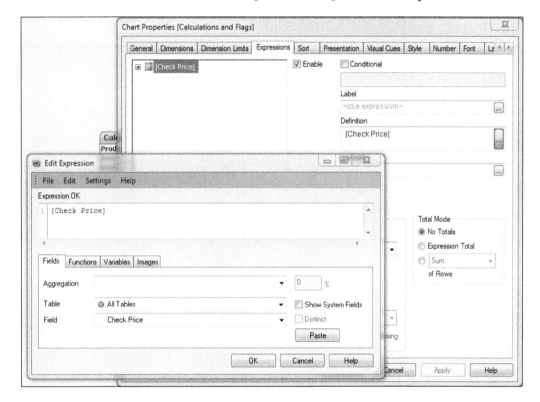

We still suppress zero values and hide the column:

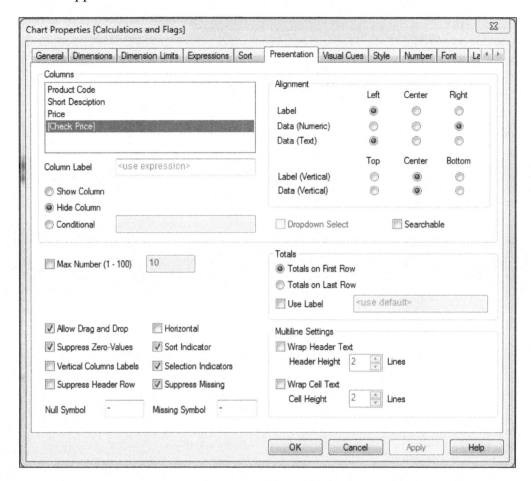

You can use this technique when a chart is noticeably slow to perform on screen. Using flags makes Set Analysis easier too.

Check how long each object takes to calculate by opening **Document Properties** and clicking on the **Sheets** tab. **Calc Time** shows, in milliseconds, how long each object takes. (In the following example, it's zero as there are just 23 rows output!)

Chapter 6

> One thing to note here is that the results of expressions are cached, so you need to view **Sheet Properties** directly after you have loaded the form. Otherwise, **Calc Time** will be dramatically lower as QlikView will use the cache for most of its results.

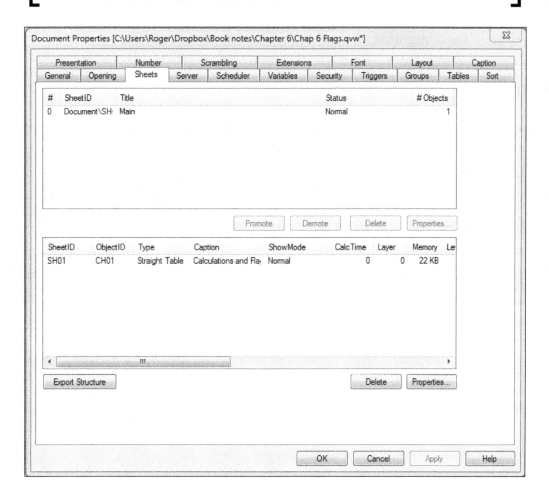

Previous() and Peek() functions

Within the scripting language, there are two functions that appear to do the same thing. These are the `Previous()` and `Peek()` functions. However, there is a subtle difference between the two when it comes to the script, and it is not just the number of parameters.

The `Peek()` function has a lot more parameters and can be used outside a `Load` statement as well, but this is not the issue here.

The following two statements work in exactly the same way:

```
if(Previous([Manufacturer No])=[Manufacturer No],1) as SameManuf
```

```
if(Peek('Manufacturer No')=[Manufacturer No],1) as  SameManuf
```

Both check to see if the previous record had the same `Manufacturer No` value (as long as data is sorted in this field). However, if we want to make a counter field, we can only use the `Peek()` function as the `Previous()` function must be used to refer to a field that actually exists in the source data.

Take a look at this statement:

```
if(Peek('Manufacturer No')=[Manufacturer No],
Peek('ManufCounter')+1, 1) as ManufCounter,
```

Here, we use `Peek()` to check for the same `Manufacturer No` value, and if this is true, we will add 1 to the last `ManufCounter` field. If the initial test is false, we will begin the counter from 1 again. As `ManufCounter` is not currently in the source data structure, we cannot use the `Previous()` function for this; however, we could use the `Previous()` function to test for the same manufacturer as this field does exist in the structure:

```
if(Previous([Manufacturer No])=[Manufacturer No],
Peek('ManufCounter')+1, 1) as ManufCounter,
```

Note that we still have to use the `Peek()` function for the counter field.

If there is no `ManufCounter` field in existence (as in the case of the very first record), the `Peek()` function will return a null.

Preceding load on preceding load

Within the QlikView scripting language, there is the ability to write Load statements on top of each other; such statements are known as **preceding loads**. This is quite a useful feature as it allows additional script to be applied without a lot of extra work.

However, there is quite a bit of processing overhead involved when you use this feature, and in most cases, it is more efficient to reload the table again (using resident) than it is to use preceding load on preceding load. Alternatively, if the reason for the preceding load on preceding load is to reuse a calculated field, it can be more efficient to reproduce the calculation again.

Consider the following example:

```
Product_Source:
LOAD *,
  Price + VAT as TotalPrice
;
LOAD [Product Code],
     Price,
     Price * 0.20 as VAT
FROM
```

Here, we calculated the VAT figure, stored it as a field, and then in the next part of the LOAD, we added the VAT figure to the price, giving us a TotalPrice field. This is fairly straightforward, but can be very inefficient at load time. It is a lot more efficient to have the following instead:

```
Product_Source:
LOAD [Product Code],
     Price,
     Price * 0.20 as VAT,
     Price + (Price * 0.20) as TotalPrice
FROM
```

This version does the same calculation again but executes it a lot faster. It would appear that there is quite an overhead in processing time when preceding load on preceding load is used; so, unless you have to do many calculations, try to avoid it.

An alternative approach would be to load the table again using a *resident* statement in a new table and finally dropping the source, as follows:

```
Product_Source_A:
LOAD [Product Code],
     Price,
     Price * 0.20 as VAT
FROM
[..\QlikView Unlocked Data.xlsx]
(ooxml, embedded labels, table is Product);

Product_Source:
NoConcatenate
LOAD *,
   Price + VAT as TotalPrice
Resident Product_Source_A;

DROP Table Product_Source_A;
```

This assumes that you have enough memory to load the table again. It would be wise to check the timings of the two approaches to see which is more efficient in your environment.

Finding min and max

One of the standard pieces of script that tends to be used over and over again is the creation of a `Master Calendar` table. The first stage of this is to find the date range, from minimum to maximum, from your fact table and create all the possible days in between. In fact, this is even part of the main QlikView Developers' training course. We looked at this in *Chapter 5, The Right Data Model Pays Dividends*, when we created our Data Island.

The normal way to find the minimum and maximum dates is to use a piece of script such as this:

```
TempDates:
LOAD Min([Order Date]) as MinDate,
     Max([Order Date]) as MaxDate
Resident SalesOrders;
```

```
LET varMinDate=peek('MinDate',0,'TempDates');
LET varMaxDate=peek('MaxDate',0,'TempDates');

DROP Table TempDates;
```

Here, we created a one record table with the minimum and maximum values as separate fields and then used `Peek` on the resulting table to get the values.

This is fine if we only have a couple of thousand rows; however, when we talk about millions of rows from a large fact table, this script can take many minutes to execute.

Consider this piece of script:

```
TempDates:
LOAD FieldValue('Order Date',IterNo()) as OrderDate
   AutoGenerate 1 While not IsNull(FieldValue('Order Date',IterNo())) ;

TempDates_2:
LOAD Min(OrderDate) as MinDate,
     Max(OrderDate) as MaxDate
Resident TempDates;

LET varMinDate=peek('MinDate',0,'TempDates_2');
LET varMaxDate=peek('MaxDate',0,'TempDates_2');

DROP Tables TempDates, TempDates_2;
```

Although the script is longer and uses two temporary tables, it executes a lot faster — in most cases, in seconds.

This script works by reading the internal memory table for the `Order Date` field and only creates a record for each unique occurrence as that is all that is held in memory. This means that for a range of 10 years, the maximum number of records would be 3,653. From this, finding the minimum and maximum is extremely quick.

Autonumber

Although the most efficient data model is a single flat file, this is rarely possible, and we need to have linked tables. This means that we will have at least one linking field. In most cases, this field is not presented to the user as it is likely to be code or a combination of fields.

In this case, we can take advantage of the `Autonumber()` function. Rather than storing the contents of the field in memory, it stores the internal pointer to this particular occurrence of the field content. We have also noticed that sometimes the pointer is only stored in the record header and not as a separate field, therefore saving a lot of space; however, this is not always the case.

This is especially useful if you have to create a key field (by combining individual fields) to avoid synthetic keys, as these can be extremely large and, by their use, completely unique.

Unfortunately there is a downside; in this case, it comes with a performance hit. We are back to our old friend, the Time/Space Compromise. At least the hit is in running the script and not the execution of the document. In fact, the document should run faster as the memory requirement is less.

Reading from a spreadsheet

There are times when we need to read data from an Excel spreadsheet, and in many cases, this data comes from a single worksheet inside it. The QlikView wizard creates something similar to this:

```
FROM
[..\QlikView Unlocked Data Chapter 4.xlsx]
(ooxml, embedded labels, table is [Sheet1]);
```

This is fine, but if the user decides to tidy up the spreadsheet and give the worksheet a name, it will stop the script from running. However, if we remove the ", table is [Sheet1]" part, it will still work fine:

```
FROM
[..\QlikView Unlocked Data Chapter 4.xlsx]
(ooxml, embedded labels);
```

This would happen as long as the data is still on the first worksheet. This just builds in a little extra bit of resilience.

You can also read multiple files using a wildcard in the name. This works with all types of files, including database tables. So, for example, you might have spreadsheets with sales data in them for each month and year. The names of each spreadsheet could be something similar to `Sales 2014-01.xlsx`, `Sales 2014-02.xlsx`, and so on. You could read them all with a single statement, such as this:

```
FROM
[..\Sales *.xlsx]
(ooxml, embedded labels);
```

Just ensure that they all have the same field names!

Summary

In this chapter, we departed from the style of previous chapters by presenting a number of our favorite time-saving performance tips and tricks without the background reasons for them. Most developers encounter situations sooner or later where these tips are invaluable and save time and effort.

7
Improving Chart Performance and Usability

In this chapter, we will cover the following key topics:

- Don't forget screen performance
- Cached expressions
- Multiple selection criteria
- Copying expressions
- Reusing chart expressions
- Hidden graphics
- Making charts more readable
- Helping the user – Help Text
- Resizing objects
- Stopping objects from being moved
- Defaulting the scroll bar to the right of a chart

Don't forget screen performance

It's all well and good to have a visually stunning document, but if its performance is poor, user experience will suffer greatly. In this chapter, we will not try to teach you how to design visually impressive charts—that's a whole other book; instead, we will offer some ideas to help make your charts work better.

Improving Chart Performance and Usability

> A rule of thumb is that nothing should take longer than about 3 seconds to refresh as this is the point at which the user gets bored.

Here are some performance tips to enhance the overall user experience by taking advantage of QlikView's excellent server engine and other features.

Cached expressions

One of the ways to get a stunning performance from the QlikView engine is to cache all its expression results for each selection made (well, all that will fit in available memory, that is).

> If you Google the definition of cache, you'll get something similar to this:
> *Noun: cache*
> *"Computers: A temporary storage space or memory that allows fast access to data".*

This means that every time an expression needs to be recalculated, the cache is used to check whether the same expression has been used with the current selection criteria. If it has, the result is taken from the cache rather than being recalculated again. However, take a look at these three expressions:

- Sum(TotalPrice)
- sum(TotalPrice)
- sum (TotalPrice)

All the three expressions stated here give exactly the same result, but each is executed and cached individually. This is because there are subtle differences in each: the second and third have a lowercase "s" in the Sum function, and the third also has a space between the Sum and open parenthesis.

Each has its own cache entry and result store but is calculated individually. If all three expressions were exactly the same (it doesn't matter which), only one would be calculated and the other two would have their results taken from the cache.

The same rule applies to what is inside the parenthesis as well. Luckily, field names have to be case-specific, but adding spaces in the expression to make it more readable can make a difference. This is not a bad thing; just keep your code consistent.

The point, then, is to always write your expressions in exactly the same way throughout your document or put common expressions in a variable. (We also mentioned this in *Chapter 3, Are You Sitting Comfortably? Be More Productive*.) Copy and paste expression formulae in order to achieve consistency.

Multiple selection criteria

When a document is being used, the user usually wants to make a number of selections before evaluating the results. For example, he/she may choose a period, then a client, and finally a product.

This is all well and good, but each time they make one of these selections, the whole screen is recalculated. If you have a document with many rows of data and complex expressions (especially those with Set Analysis overriding selection criteria), it can take a while, meaning that the user is left waiting before they make the next selection.

One way we can help reduce the waiting time is to use one of QlikView's performance enhancements. It doesn't refresh objects that are *hidden*. So, how do we do it? The following steps will help:

1. Create a variable and set it to zero.
2. Make your major object only visible on the content of a variable that is set to zero.
3. Create a button that toggles this variable between one and zero.
4. Make a selection panel that is also only visible on the content of a variable but this time when the variable is set to one.

In more detail: select **Variable Overview** from the **Settings** menu and add a new variable, something similar to the following screenshot:

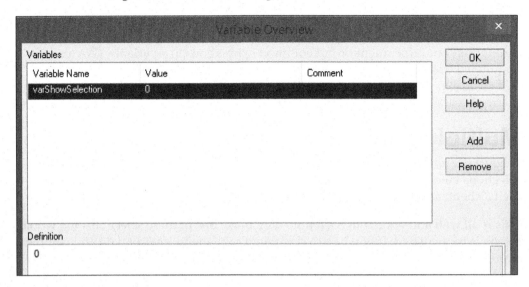

Give it a definition of zero. Edit the properties of your object, and on the **Layout** tab, change the **Show** option to **Conditional**. The condition contains our variable equal to zero:

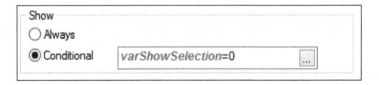

Add a **Button** object with a text of something similar to Show / Hide Selection and add the following action:

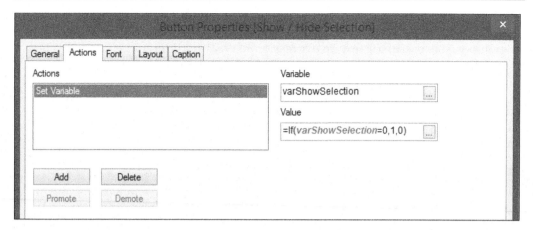

> You could also write this as 1 - varShowSelection to avoid the need for an IF() statement.

Now, when we press the button, the objects should disappear, and then they should reappear when we press it again. If we really want to be smart, we could alter the **Text** property of our button to:

```
=if(varShowSelection=0,'Show','Hide') & ' Selection'
```

This way, the **Text** button will change from **Show Selection** to **Hide Selection**, depending on what is viewed.

If you now press the button to hide the objects, there will be a space in the document where you can add the selection objects. On each of the object properties, set the **Show** property to **Conditional** with the following value:

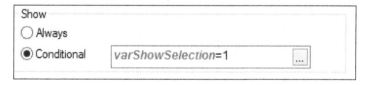

Once we have added all the selection objects, we can press the button object again. This time, the selections will be hidden, and the chart objects will become visible. These will now be refreshed with our current selection, but at least it is only a single time.

Copying expressions

Sometimes, it is useful to copy an expression to create a different version. This is especially useful if you have expressions in background color, text color, or text format as all of these are copied too.

For those who have never used this feature, right-click on an existing expression in the **Expressions** tab of object properties, and you will see the following submenu appear:

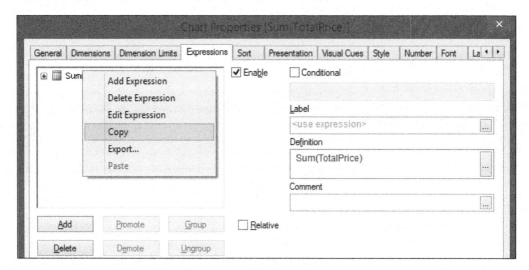

Click on **Copy**, then move the cursor to an empty part of the **Expressions** list, and right-click again; this time, this submenu will appear:

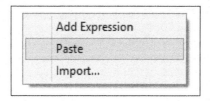

Clicking on **Paste** will create a copy of your expression, which will be added at the bottom of the list. You can now edit it.

Reusing chart expressions

We have mentioned this previously. If you need to do repeated calculations, it is better to do these in the script and create extra fields there. However, there are times when this may not be possible. One way that would appear to solve this issue when using a **Chart** object is to use a previously calculated **Label** expression in other expressions.

On the surface, this would appear to be more efficient, and it certainly makes the script easier to read; in practice, there is no speed advantage, and in most tests, it works slightly more slowly. It is, therefore, more efficient to duplicate this part of the expression again.

Have a look at this simple example:

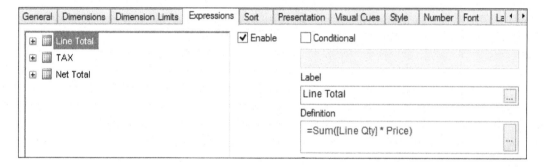

Here, to show the TAX figure, we will use the following expression:

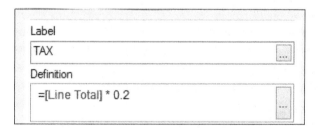

However, it would be more efficient to use this expression instead:

```
=Sum([Line Qty] * Price) * 0.2
```

Hidden graphics

Every graphic and icon used on the QlikView desktop is available for you without any overhead of storing the image. In fact, there are over 450 such images. For those of you that used the early version of Word for Windows, you might remember Mr. Clippy, the animated icon for help. He is also one of these embedded images, although he is not animated:

Create a text box, and place the following in the text field:

```
qmem://<bundled>/Images/clippy.png
```

Then, set the **Representation** value to **Image**, and then as if by magic, Mr. Clippy will appear. A full list and examples of these hidden images are given in *Appendix, Hidden Image List*.

Making charts more readable

Occasionally, we have used Borchester Models' data to demonstrate certain ideas and features. Have a look at this script fragment:

```
Stock:
LOAD [Shop No],
     [Product Code],
     [On Hand]
FROM
[QlikView Unlocked Data.xlsx]
(ooxml, embedded labels, table is Stock);
```

What is required here is a chart showing stock levels by product across all shops. However, if we just let QlikView do the sorting, it will use **Product Code**, and we will see something similar to this:

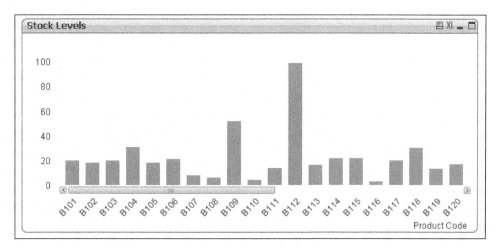

This is okay, but it's not really helpful. As there's a scroll bar, we can't see what we have the most stock of—it might be **B112**, but unless we scroll across, we won't know. Furthermore, it is hard to determine the relative differences between the stock levels of other products.

To make this much more readable, we just need to make a simple change in the properties of the chart object on the **Sort** tab, as follows:

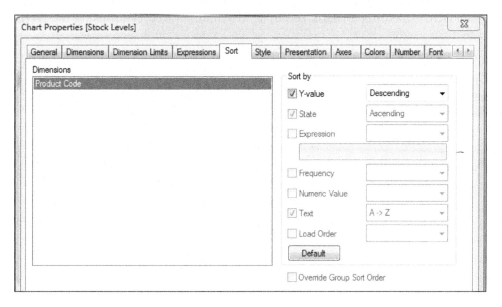

By simply changing the sort to **Y-value** (and in this case, using the default **Descending** option), we can make the chart much easier to interpret, as shown in the following graph:

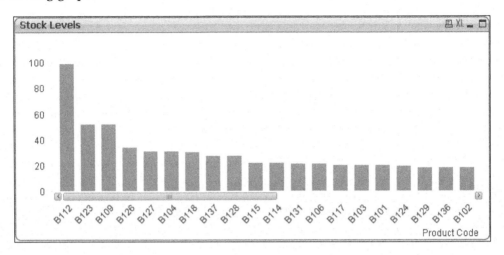

Using this technique in the appropriate places can help make your charts and tables even more useful and intuitive.

Helping the user – Help Text

Although QlikView is very intuitive and easy for users to understand, sometimes the user needs extra help. If your application uses some complex calculations or it isn't obvious why something is displayed in a particular way, consider using the **Help Text** feature.

The **Help Text** feature is very useful. You may be asked to write a user manual for an application—we think you should resist this at all costs. QlikView is much too dynamic for printed user application manuals. Use the **Help Text** instead, and just update the text when you change or create an object.

Chapter 7

The **Help Text** is found on the **Caption** tab of object properties on the lower right-hand side:

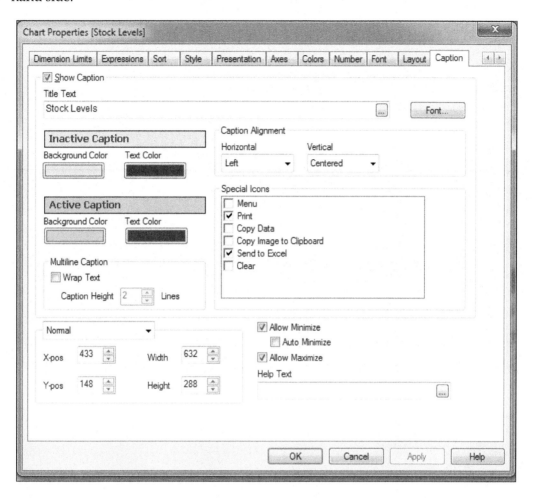

Improving Chart Performance and Usability

Clicking on the **...** button brings up the usual **Edit Expression** box, where you can write your help text, as shown in the following screenshot:

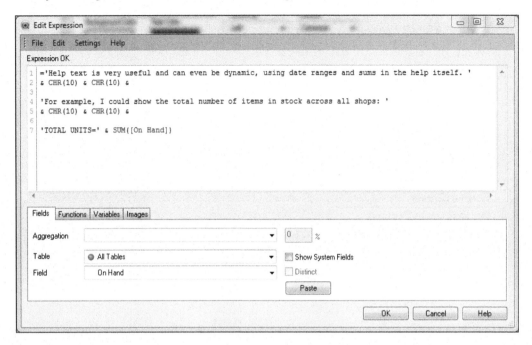

After saving the **Help Text**, if you click on the question mark icon in the top right corner of the chart object, you'll see something similar to this:

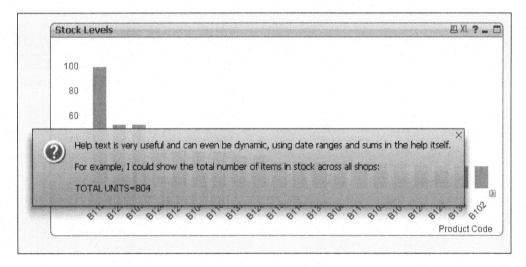

Just moving the mouse over the question mark will display **Help** as a tooltip, but clicking on the question mark will keep help on the screen until you close it.

Use this feature to explain complex calculations, Set Analysis, and so on to your user, and you'll never need to write a user manual again.

Resizing objects

Once you have designed your application, got all the objects in the right place, and it's all looking good, spare a bit of time to ensure that the actual size specified for each object is correct.

As your document stands, you may have list boxes showing all possible entries without scroll bars, but over time, these may increase in size, causing them to scroll, or worse still, overlap other objects. Also, if your users access the document particularly with an AJAX client, sometimes grey boxes are shown as the document is drawn. These grey boxes are the full size of an object, and this may look messy if objects overlap.

Avoiding both of these issues is very straightforward. First of all, select the **Design Grid** option from the **View** menu. This not only makes the layout grid visible, but also enables the next step. Now, click on each object in turn. As you do so, you will notice a box placed around the total size of the object, irrespective of the size actually used. This black box is the maximum space the object will use, as illustrated in the following screenshot:

If there is a chance of overlapping objects, use the place holders at the bottom or to the right and make the black box smaller.

> One quirk with QlikView is that the black box does not shrink. To see how much you have changed the size, click on a different object and then click back on the original again to make the change visible.

Stopping objects from being moved

Once the application is on the server and left in the hands of the user, things may move around the screen as users try to make selections, and they may inadvertently move the object or resize it. You can avoid this by performing the following steps.

First, here's the long way round:

1. Press *Ctrl + Shift +S* at the same time to show all hidden objects.
2. Press *Ctrl + A* to select all the objects on the sheet.
3. Right-click on one object and select **Properties**.
4. Open the **Layout** tab; in the **Options** box, unselect **Allow Move/Size** and **Allow Copy/Clone** (refer to the following screenshot).
5. Click on **OK** to close **Properties**.
6. Press *Ctrl + Shift + S* at the same time to hide the hidden objects.
7. Repeat the procedure for each tab of your document.

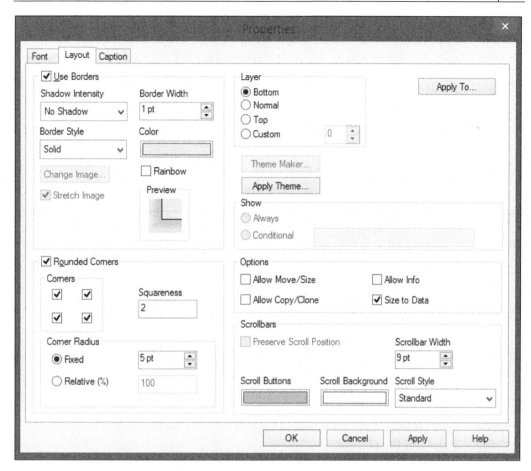

Alternatively, you can achieve the same effect by just unselecting the **Move/Size Objects** option in the **Security** tab of **Sheet Properties**. This will affect the whole document in one go.

Improving Chart Performance and Usability

Here's another alternative: if you have access to QlikView Management Console, unselect the **Allow Moving and Sizing Objects** option on the **System | Setup | Documents** tab for the server, which is, of course, a global setting for all documents.

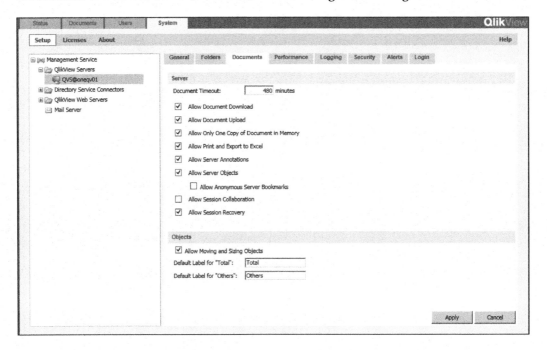

Whichever you choose, your users won't be able to mess up the screen by moving, resizing, or copying the objects.

It's also worth unselecting the **Allow Minimize** and **Allow Maximize** options on the **Caption** tab of an object, especially if the object needs to always appear on screen. If you are to show and hide objects using buttons, you should always unselect these options.

Defaulting the scroll bar to the right of a chart

There are times when you have a lot of dimensions and a scroll bar is required. However, suppose you want to sort on date, going from the oldest to newest, and you want to make the default view the current one, which shows the newest dates that are on the right-hand side of the chart. There is no obvious property that allows this. However, there is a property built into the chart object; it's just that there isn't a GUI option to set it.

The way to set this property is to write a subroutine in the Module script and then to run it just once.

In the example elaborated earlier in this chapter, where we sorted a chart's dimensions, we can show this with the scroll bar to the right.

First of all, we need the **Object ID** of the chart that we wish to change. Open up the properties and look at the **General** tab. To the right is a box with the **Object ID**; in this case, it is CH02:

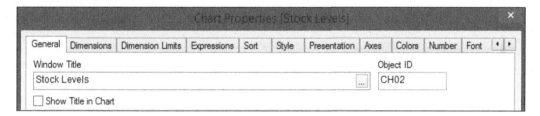

Now, we need to add the following text to the Module script. First, open the **Edit Module** window from the **Tools** menu and then enter the following:

You will notice the CH02 parameter in the GetSheetObject function; this is the **Object ID** from the previous screenshot.

Once the text has been entered, click on the **Check** button on the upper left-hand side. If everything is okay, the **RightAlign** function name will appear below the check button.

To execute this piece of code, click on the **RightAlign** text in the list box on the left-hand side and then press the **Test** button below it.

Nothing will appear to happen, but this is quite normal. Click on the **OK** button to end the **Edit Module** window and save the document. If you close your document and open it again, you will see that the chart is now showing the right of the dimension list:

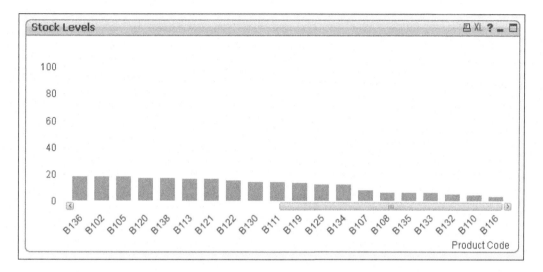

This process needs to be repeated for each object you wish to set the **Right Align** property to.

Summary

In this chapter, we again departed from the style of chapters 1 to 5. We showed you a number of tips that will help improve the performance of your charts and make them even easier for your users to work with.

8
To Deployment and Beyond

This chapter will cover the following key topics:

- Security and Section Access
- Why server jobs fail
- Deploying from development to UAT and on to production
- The golden source
- Why Publisher isn't always a good thing
- Your two best friends
- It will never be perfect but it will be close

Security and Section Access

Sometimes we need to make sure that only certain users can view all or part of a document.

Explanation

We may want to limit the use of our document to certain people or restrict the rows of information individuals can see or even which fields a user can view. QlikView has the ability to restrict all of these.

Although security is a major part of our application, it should be considered as part of the initial data design. However, it may be easier to add security once the document is established.

Background

One of the best ways of securing a document is to use the Section Access facility. There are a number of functions within this, which are described in the following section. However, for simple security tasks, we can leave out Section Access and control security manually.

How to do it

We have a number of options to choose from for security. First of all, let's take a look at who can use the document without having to implement QlikView's Section Access.

Physical Network Access

You can restrict the read permission of the QVW file on your server. If a user cannot see the QVW file, QlikView won't let them access it (by NTFS authorization).

If you are not using Small Business Edition QlikView Server, you also have the option of DMS authorization, which allows you to specify which users can access the document via QlikView's QMC.

Document CALs

If your QlikView Server uses Document CALs, then unless you assign one to a user, they will not be able to open the document as long as you have **Allow dynamic CAL assignment** unselected.

> Remember that named users will also have access as they don't need individual CALs, and you could unintentionally grant access to documents they should not see.

With Publisher

If your QlikView Server has the Publisher extension, you can select named users in the **User Type** option of the distribution task, where you can specify the users who can open the document. This could be a local or active directory security group.

Once you control who can open the document, you might want to control what a specific list of users can see. This can either be a positive or negative list; for example, you may want to show something to specific people or hide something from those in a list.

[Remember that it is better to fail safe and make it a positive list (which means that those in the list can see certain information).]

You can have a table of users (this could come from an inline list, a spreadsheet, or a database table). For these examples, we will assume that the table contains a list of users in a field called `AccessUserNames`. First, we will create a variable (`varUserAccess`) that contains the following expression:

```
='#' & Concat(Upper(AccessUserNames),'#') & '#'
```

This will create a single string containing all the usernames, separated by # and in uppercase. We added the # sign to the beginning and the end so that we can identify exact matches of usernames without the fear of getting a submatch. To use this list, we now need to add the following to the **Conditional Show** property of the object we wish to protect:

```
index(varUserAccess , '#' & Upper(OSUser()) & '#' )  >0
```

The preceding uses the `OSUser()` function to return the current user's full network ID, so it is essential that the original user list contains the network domain name as well as the user ID (for example, `Domain\User1`). If a match is found, this condition will be true, so the object (be it a button, chart, chart column, or even sheet) will be visible.

To make this feature a bit more efficient, we could set the variable to the concatenation in the script rather than relying on the variable to be recalculated every time a selection is performed. We could use something along the lines of the following:

```
TempTable:
Load
  Concat(Upper(AccessUserNames),'#') as Temp
Resident UserList;

LET varUserAccess ='#' & Peek('Temp',0) & '#' ;

DROP Table TempTable;
```

This is just a basic example to demonstrate the concept. This method can be used in numerous ways with multiple variables to have a number of different restrictions applied. Always remember to ensure that you, as a developer, are included in the list so that you can access the function as a user would.

Section Access

Now, let's move on to Section Access—what is it? It is a part of the script used to generate a security model, which controls:

- Who has access to the document
- Which rows they can see (Data Reduction)
- Which fields they can't see (OMIT fields)

You can specify the "who" factor through:

- A network ID
- The QlikView serial number
- A Windows NT Domain SID
- A Windows NT SID
- Manually entered username and password

If you have multiple types defined, QlikView will check the preceding types in this order.

Be careful if you are using a serial number or either of the Windows SIDs as changing network settings or servers could lock you out; so, it would be a good idea to have a hidden username and password option.

The **Help** section in QlikView has a good description and examples of all the options—look for **Security** in the **Index** search. For further reading, there is also a Qlik white paper on Section Access.

Section Access applies to every way of opening the document, whether it be from the server or by the desktop edition. All restrictions are enforced. Because of this, it is easy when developing to make a mistake that locks you out of the document, and there is no way back in.

Make plenty of backups, especially one before you start to develop the Section Access code.

First of all, we want to use Section Access to control who can see the document. By adding the following script, QlikView will automatically restrict access to those in the list; in fact, anyone not in the list will not even see the document in QlikView Access Point:

```
SECTION Access;

USERS:
LOAD * INLINE [
    ACCESS,     NTNAME
    ADMIN,      DOMAIN\QLIKVIEW
    ADMIN,      DOMAIN\DEVELOPER1
    USER,       DOMAIN\PERSON1
];

SECTION Application;
```

The `SECTION Access` statement defines the start of the special script, and the `SECTION Application` statement reverts it back to normal.

> This code can appear at any part of your script, but more often, it is placed at the beginning or even in **Hidden Script** tabs for extra security. (Just ensure that you remember the password!)

One important fact to raise at this point is that everything within Section Access must be in uppercase; this includes field names as well as the content of the fields.

> It is easier if the network account that is running the QlikView Distribution Service on the server is included in the user list as the server must be able to open the document to reload it. If you have a Test server in your infrastructure, you need to ensure that you have access to the service account name running the QlikView server on the test machine as well as the production machine so that the documents can be refreshed on the appropriate servers.

In this script, there are only three users that will be able to open this document. `QlikView` and `Developer1` are both assigned Administrator privileges (we will come to this later in this section). `Person1` is classified as a standard user. The Distribution Service account user (QlikView in the preceding example) should have administrator privileges.

To Deployment and Beyond

We used the NTNAME field to specify our "who" list. This is the network ID field, including the domain name, but we could use any of the "who" fields mentioned before.

When you reload the document with Section Access in place, you will not see the USERS table in the **View Table** option as it is always hidden. Furthermore, it will not be included in any memory statistics output (we will discuss this later in this chapter).

At this stage, it is worth saving the document once the reload is finished and then opening it again in another instance of QlikView (do not close the current instance). If the document fails to open, you still have the chance to rectify issues in the current instance as QlikView checks Section Access when you open the document but doesn't check once it is open.

The next phase of Section Access is Data Reduction, which will automatically reduce the number of rows available to a user depending on the content of the Section Access table. There is no way for a user to override the facility, so it provides a very secure application. Data Reduction is optional, so if you only want to restrict access, you don't need Data Reduction.

However, if you wish to use Data Reduction, there should be a link between the table created within Section Access and the main data model. This has the effect of making an unclearable selection of this field when the document is loaded by a user.

For the sake of this chapter, we will assume that our data model is rather simple and looks similar to this:

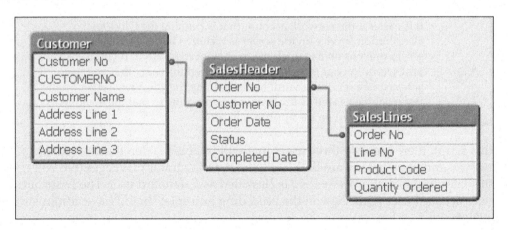

This is very straightforward; it's just a Customer list with Sales Header and Lines tables.

We'll make a small change to our Section Access script, as follows:

```
SECTION Access;

STAR is *;

USERS:
LOAD * INLINE [
    ACCESS,     NTNAME,             CUSTOMERNO
    ADMIN,      DOMAIN\QLIKVIEW,    *
    ADMIN,      DOMAIN\DEVELOPER1,  1001
    USER,       DOMAIN\PERSON1,     1002
];

SECTION Application;
```

We added an additional column, CUSTOMERNO, to our USERS table. You will notice that in the table view, there is also a CUSTOMERNO field in the Customer table. This creates a link between the USERS access table and the Customers table.

There is also an additional line added that defines which character is to be used as a wildcard. The STAR is *; line defines * the character as the wildcard. This means that in the above example, a QlikView user will have access to all records, whereas Developer1 will only see customer 1001, and Person1 will only see 1002.

> The user will see all the records that feature in this field within the Section Access table. In this example, if there was also a CUSTOMERNO 1003, Developer1 and Person1 would not see it.

If you were Developer1, then after a reload, you would notice you can see all the records because Data Reduction is not applied until you reopen the document.

If you want Person1 to have access to two or more Customers, you can simply add additional lines into the table with the extra CUSTOMERNO.

> Having a second instance of QlikView running is useful to test security as you can use the second instance to check without closing the one you are working on.

There is, however, one more thing we need to do before Data Reduction will work, and that is to turn it on.

In **Document Properties**, from the **Settings** menu, click on the **Opening** tab:

Halfway down, you will see **Initial Data Reduction Based on Section Access**. Select this box and ensure that **Strict Exclusion** is also selected. It is wise to select the **Prohibit Binary Load** option as well, as this prevents any other QlikView developers from accessing the data model.

Now, everything is in place for the reduction to work, but we can take security one step further. Still in **Document Properties**, move to the **Security** tab:

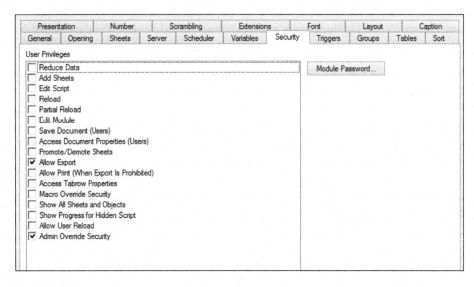

Chapter 8

Now, unselect everything except **Allow Export** (unless you specifically don't want the user to be able to export) and select **Admin Override Security**.

In the preceding script, we defined people as either ADMIN or USERS. This is where we can define what a USER can and cannot do and also allow ADMIN users access to everything.

 Ensure that you keep **Admin Override Security** on if you create any other USER restrictions; otherwise, you, as an ADMIN user, will not be able to perform these functions.

Hiding fields

We have restricted users and removed rows of data from our users. Now, we want to look at removing specific fields from specific users as well.

To do this, we will add the OMIT field to the script. If we want to hide the Status column from the Person1 user, we could change the script to:

```
USERS:
LOAD * INLINE [
    ACCESS,     NTNAME,                 CUSTOMERNO,   OMIT
    ADMIN,      DOMAIN\QLIKVIEW,        *,
    ADMIN,      DOMAIN\DEVELOPER1,      1001,
    USER,       DOMAIN\PERSON1,         1002,     Status
];
```

Here, we did not provide an OMIT line to our Server or Developer Accounts. If we wanted to have a number of fields hidden, we would need to repeat the USERS row with a different field name. This could become quite unmanageable as we may have multiple rows for a user because of multiple selections. To overcome this, we could adopt a different approach, as follows:

```
USERS:
LOAD * INLINE [
    ACCESS,     NTNAME,                 CUSTOMERNO,   OMITTYPE
    ADMIN,      DOMAIN\QLIKVIEW,        *,
    ADMIN,      DOMAIN\DEVELOPER1,      1001,
    USER,       DOMAIN\PERSON1,         1002,     2
];

OMITFIELDS:
LOAD * INLINE [
    OMITTYPE, OMIT
```

To Deployment and Beyond

```
      1, Status
      2, Status
      2, 'Quantity Ordered'
];
```

Here, we created a second table with the OMIT field in it, linking it to the main USERS table with an additional field. A user with an OMITTYPE value of 1 will have the Status field hidden, one with a value of 2 will have both the Status and Quantity Ordered fields hidden, and one with no value will have neither field hidden.

> Where a field name has a space within, it should be enclosed within single quotation marks. Wildcard characters can also be used.

> One thing to bear in mind when using the OMIT function is never to OMIT a key field as this will stop the linking of tables within your data model and probably cause some strange, unexpected results.

Passing additional parameters

So far, we provided a mechanism to control which rows and fields a user is able to see. However, there are times when we want to control other objects, be it a chart, table, or even a complete sheet.

Consider this script:

```
SECTION Access;

STAR is *;

USERS:
LOAD * INLINE [
      ACCESS,    NTNAME,              CUSTOMERNO,   OPTION1,   OPTION2
      ADMIN,     DOMAIN\QLIKVIEW,     *,            YES,       YES
      ADMIN,     DOMAIN\DEVELOPER1,   1001,         YES,       NO
      USER,      DOMAIN\PERSON1,      1002,         YES,       YES
];
```

```
SECTION Application;

Option1List:
LOAD * INLINE [
    OPTION1, Option1
    YES,    Yes
    NO,     No
];

Option2List:
LOAD * INLINE [
    OPTION2, Option2
    YES,    Yes
    NO,     No
];
```

Notice the two additional fields, OPTION1 and OPTION2, in our USERS table. There are also two additional tables under Section Application in the script, which link these two fields. These two tables will become data islands when the document is reloaded.

When our Development1 user opens this document, the two new data island tables will only contain one record in each: Option1 being Yes and Option2 being No.

We can now add a conditional Show property to any object that we want to control with this option, as follows:

```
Option1='Yes'
```

This principle can be used for as many options as you need.

Directly after a reload, as a developer, we need to save our document, close it, and then reopen it so that Data Reduction is applied. Otherwise, all data island tables will contain all the records and conditional views will all resolve to "false".

Section Access with Data Reduction and QlikView Publisher

If you have QlikView Publisher installed on your server, you might encounter the following message whenever anyone tries to open your document after it has been reloaded and distributed:

This happens because after a reload, the QlikView server opens the reloaded document from the Source folder and saves it in the Users folder. However, if Data Reduction is applied, the document is loaded with the server account's restrictions and then subsequently saved with only the server account user in the table. However, there is a way around this, which is to not give the QlikView Server account access to any records. For some reason, this solves the issue. In our preceding script, we would have a line similar to the following:

```
USERS:
LOAD * INLINE [
    ACCESS,   NTNAME,         CUSTOMERNO
    ADMIN,    DOMAIN\QLIKVIEW,
```

Simply remove * so that the field is null.

Section Access can be a very powerful part of your document. Don't be put off by the severity of the warnings. However, we suggest that you have a play with a simple document before you add it to a live document for the first time and keep lots of backups when you do this.

> Remember that the security section of QlikView Help is a good reference.

Why server jobs fail

There are many reasons why jobs fail on a server; here are a few of the common ones and ideas on how to avoid them. Also, ensure that your document has the **Generate Log File** option selected in the **General** tab of **Document Properties** as this makes identifying the issue a lot easier. The default log file created by QlikView Server is rarely of any help, but the document log file gives us more helpful error messages at approximately the script line that failed.

Connection failures

If you are connected to a database using OLE DB, you have the option of supplying a username and password for database access. One common failure here is that the password may have expired. It is better to set up your connection to use the NT authentication and have the account running the QlikView Distribution service added to the database list of authenticated users. (Only read access is required most of the time.)

Excel spreadsheets

There are many reasons why these fail, but most of them are due to the user changing the layout after the application has been written.

If your spreadsheet has only one worksheet, remove the `table is` option from the `From` entry in the script. Then, should the user change the worksheet's name, the document will still reload.

Make a copy of the column field names on the row beneath the existing one and hide this row. Alter your load script to use this hidden row as your script's fields. The user can then alter what he/she sees as column names without it affecting the layout because QlikView will use a hidden row.

Alternatively, you could use Excel's **Protect Worksheet** facility to lock the header records and stop users from deleting the existing columns, but ensure that you store the password used (a comment in your script may be a good place).

Another common reason for spreadsheets failing to load is the file's version. As you almost certainly know, more recent versions of Excel suffix workbook names with `.xlsx`, whereas older versions simply used `.xls`. If a user opens an older version of a spreadsheet and decides, for some reason, to save it in the new format, your load script will fail. We have lost count of the times that we have seen this happen, but it's certainly a powerful argument for going through all those old spreadsheets, upgrading them, and of course, modifying all the QVW files that use them.

> Note that changing a QVW file to use xlsx rather than xls isn't just a case of changing the filename. Excel uses different storage formats too – try using the wizard to load data from an xls and xlsx and compare the results.

Drive letters

When referring to files (QVD, TXT, XLSX, CSV, or any other type), try to use a relative path. However, if they are stored on a shared drive or network device, don't rely on a network drive mapping to be consistent. It is better to use the full URL to the file; for example:

```
\\QlikView1\ShareFolder\Data\QlikView Unlocked Data.xlsx
```

> Take care! A Windows user must have permission to access all of the path and not just the shared drive; otherwise, this will fail.

QlikView engines

When QlikView runs scheduled jobs on the server, it allocates an engine to each job as it runs. If you have more jobs attempting to start or running than you have engines available, one or more jobs will fail.

> The number of running jobs should not exceed number of engines minus 1.

We haven't found a foolproof way to determine which job(s) will fail but there are two things you can do to avoid this problem.

In the QMC, go to the **Performance** tab for the server and check the **Max Current Reloads** box. This is the maximum number of engines that QlikView can run at the same time. If you have more scheduled jobs attempting to run or start than the figure in this box, you will have random job failures. However, just increasing this number comes with a health warning – it needs to be a maximum of one less than the number of CPUs in the system. Furthermore, if you need more than nine engines, you'll need to change the Windows **HEAP** setting. You'll find this documented in the QlikView Server Manual; the registry setting you're looking for is:

```
HKEY_LOCAL_MACHINE\System\CurrentControlSet\Control\Session Manager\SubSystems\Windows
```

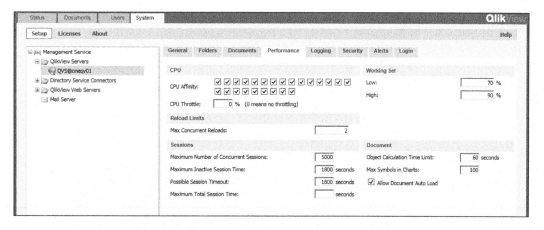

Antivirus software

Sometimes, a job may fail even though the server log says that the execution was completed successfully, and rerunning the task executes it normally. This can be due to antivirus software on the server, causing the writer of the QVW disk to fail. If you experience this problem, check out the antivirus software on your server and configure it to ignore QVW files. It is also worth mentioning that antivirus software may cause performance issues.

QVD

Attempting to overwrite an existing QVD file that is locked or on a drive without write permission can cause the script to fail.

Deploying from development to UAT and on to production

There are a few things to remember to do as your nice new document goes through testing and on into production.

Explanation

Always use a consistent approach and document it so that everyone in the team works in the same way.

Background

One of the most common reasons for applications failing when deployed to UAT or production is the fact that file paths are hardcoded.

How to do it

Keep your application in self-contained folder structures and use relative references to files used within it.

Use the same network account to run QlikView services on all machines.

If there is a need to identify which server you are running on, use the `ComputerName()` function in your script. Alternatively, you could use `$(Include=filename)` or preferably `$(Must_Include=filename)` to set a variable.

If you use an include file, keep the name the same in all environments but change the contents as appropriate to the environment. So, for example, you may have an include file called `settings.inc` in each environment, but the settings for database connections are different in each version, pointing to the appropriate database servers. (You have test databases, right?)

Place the file one level up from the main folder structure so that it is just outside the application folder layout but still referenced by a relative path location. This way, you can have a separate file on each machine that is used by all your applications.

> Using the `Include` option allows you to create standard variables, which specify the location of the common files used by your applications.

Avoid the need to change your code when moving between environments. Sooner or later, you'll miss something and end up presenting test data in the live environment or worse.

The golden source

We've said there should be one version of the truth for data. There should be one version of the truth for your document too.

Explanation

You may not be familiar with the expression "golden source", but it's a concept you should become familiar with.

Background

Because a QlikView document contains both code and data, it is more difficult than in more traditional environments to keep track of code changes. Add the fact that it is more or less impossible to assimilate all the code and settings for a QlikView document in one place and compare them to another version of the same document, and you have something of a maintenance problem. Without the suitable tools, you would need discipline if you are going to keep a code version that you can rely on as the production version.

How to do it

I can hear you saying, "the version in production is the real, latest version". Okay, maybe it is if you strictly enforce a "no change to production code" rule. But what if it can be easily bypassed or ignored completely? How sure are you, then, that the version in production hasn't been tweaked, enhanced, or simply changed?

Keeping a version of the code that has been deployed to production is vital because version control is virtually nonexistent with QlikView. Either enforce security to the point where developers simply cannot access the production code once it is deployed, or keep a separate golden source area, where production code is kept but has to be *pulled* in order to be modified and cannot be returned without intervention, signoff, or some other process that requires more than just the developer's access.

Always use the golden source as the basis for the next modification or fix. Never rely on a version of the same document in your development or UAT environment, unless you are absolutely certain that it is identical – in other words, it has the same size and timestamp. It may sound obvious, but you should never assume that one version of a QlikView document that is the same size as another version with a different timestamp actually has exactly the same code.

You may say this is all fine, "but my document is 4GB on disk and we're short of space". In this case, remove all the data from the document and just save the QVW file without data as it will not be very big at all. You can do this by navigating to **File | Reduce Data | Remove All Values**. (You may also want to consider this if your data is highly sensitive and doesn't need to be stored in the QVW file.) Bear in mind that using this option always turns off "Always one selected value" in listbox objects as we have mentioned elsewhere.

> As an alternative, make a selection of a single item of data (preferably the lowest level available—for example, a single invoice or employee). Then, from the **Reduce Data** menu item, select the **Keep Possible Values** option. This will remove all unselected data from your document, leaving just what is selected and hopefully reducing the size of your QVW file while keeping your **Always One Selected Value** property set.

Ensure that you have a version of code that you can rely on, and never assume that the last version in development or test is the one that the users actually see.

Why Publisher isn't always a good thing

Publisher is an expensive add-on. Be sure that you really need it.

Explanation

QlikView Publisher is a powerful extension of the basic server, but it also has drawbacks.

Background

An optional addition to QlikView Server is the Publisher extension, which among other things, allows for the distribution of multiple versions of a document based on a set of data reduction rules. It also allows for QlikView reports to be e-mailed directly to users, again based on a set of data reduction rules.

One of the most useful features of Publisher is the ability to have multiple task triggers for a document reload. This allows for the construction of sophisticated triggers and job cascades. Without Publisher, a document can only have a single task trigger, restricting the options for your reload schedule.

How to do it

From a developer's point of view, having Publisher alters the data location of the final QVW document. You now have a Source and User folder structure, which means that you have to be careful when specifying runtime items, such as the graphic image files you are pointing to.

The Publisher extension is a costly addition to your server, so ensure that you really need it before purchasing it. Furthermore, once added to a server, it cannot be easily removed. In fact, the only safe way is to totally remove the entire QlikView server software from your system, delete the configuration files left after the uninstall process, then reinstall QlikView, and configure it again from scratch.

Your two best friends

Fine tune your application by using a couple of handy tools.

Explanation

When developing QlikView applications, you sometimes need a little help from your friends.

Background

There are two things you should use while fine tuning your application. One is Windows Task Manager, and the other is QlikView's Memory Statistics exporter.

How to do it

When you run a document reload, it is a good idea to have Windows Task Manager open. On the **Performance** tab, if you are running Windows 8 or above, select the **Memory** icon on the left-hand side, so that the graph shows memory use.

> To open Windows Task Manager, press *Ctrl + Shift + Esc*.

What this will show is the state of the system's memory while the reload is being performed. What you don't want to see is the line running at the top of the graph as this would indicate that you are using all of the system's memory. This means that Windows may be starting to *page* its memory, which is rather time consuming.

It is also worth viewing the Task Manager window when you test the document, as this would show whether the document is using a lot more memory than you expect.

To Deployment and Beyond

One big question that is always asked is how much memory the document is using. This is hard to quantify unless you use the second of our favorite tools: QlikView's **Memory Statistics** option.

From the **Settings** menu, select **Document Properties**; on the **General** tab, you will see a **Memory Statistics** button:

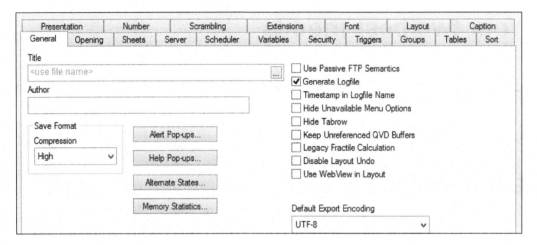

When you press the button, you are asked for the filename of the export file. This creates a CSV file with a .mem extension. This can be read by Microsoft Excel or even by another QlikView application.

The file contains a number of different statistics, but the two important ones are in the table and field, which appear lower in the **Type** column. The **Records** subtype tells you how much space is being used to store the record pointers for each table, and **Field Type** entries show how much space is being used to store each field. It also shows the number of unique entries, which can also be quite useful.

By adding all these entries together, you can see how much memory is used to store the data model.

Using the simple example from earlier in this chapter, this is how its memory statistics would look in Excel:

	A	B	C	D	E	F	G	H	I
1	Class	Type	SubType	Id	Bytes	Count	Size	CalcTime	AvgCalcTime
33	Database	Table	Records	Option1List	2	2	1		
34	Database	Table	Records	Option2List	2	2	1		
35	Database	Table	Records	Customer	10	5	2		
36	Database	Table	Records	SalesHeader	20	10	2		
37	Database	Table	Records	SalesLines	26	13	2		
47	Database	Field	Symbols	OPTION1	17	2	8.5		
48	Database	Field	Symbols	Option1	17	2	8.5		
49	Database	Field	Symbols	OPTION2	17	2	8.5		
50	Database	Field	Symbols	Option2	17	2	8.5		
51	Database	Field	Symbols	CUSTOMERNO	0	5	0		
52	Database	Field	Symbols	Customer No	0	5	0		
53	Database	Field	Symbols	Customer Name	66	5	13.2		
54	Database	Field	Symbols	Address Line 1	112	5	22.4		
55	Database	Field	Symbols	Address Line 2	43	3	14.33		
56	Database	Field	Symbols	Address Line 3	17	1	17		
57	Database	Field	Symbols	Order No	0	10	0		
58	Database	Field	Symbols	Order Date	32	4	8		
59	Database	Field	Symbols	Status	16	2	8		
60	Database	Field	Symbols	Completed Date	40	5	8		
61	Database	Field	Symbols	Line No	0	2	0		
62	Database	Field	Symbols	Product Code	110	11	10		

You will be able to obtain a lot of useful information about the storage of your application from an export such as this. If you notice the selected cell, our **CUSTOMERNO** field has five entries but takes up zero bytes. This is because the field only stores whole numbers; therefore, the pointer to the field in the **Table Type** entry can store the field value rather than a pointer to the field list, taking up less memory.

Earlier in the book, we mentioned that splitting fields can save memory but can also potentially use more memory in the long run. By looking at the **Table Entry Records** subtype, we can see the memory being used to hold the pointers. Then, by checking the **Field** symbols, we can see the memory used to store the field.

Making a **Memory Statistic** export before and after you make any modifications to your data model would give you a good indication of what effect your changes have had on memory.

> You might find it useful to make a simple QlikView application that reads the `.mem` files and has a pivot table object with the `Type` and `Id` as dimensions and sum of `Bytes` as the expression. Adding a `FileName()` function to the script would also allow you to read and compare different versions of your exports.

Memory is the key to good performance; seeing how much is used while reloading and by the document itself is a major tool to get the best out of QlikView.

It will never be perfect but it will be close

There comes a time when you have to stop developing and start deploying.

Explanation

It was once said that every project reaches 98 percent completion and stays there. Most projects eventually go live, but development is a continuous process in almost every case.

Background

So, you have built a great looking, robust, and powerful QlikView application. It's been deployed to production, it runs well, and users think you're a genius (and of course you are!). Now what? Well, there is always one more thing you can do. And one more after that.

How to do it

It is more or less inevitable that users will ask for improvements or new features when an application has been in use for a while. This may even happen within days of it going live. Business rarely stands still for long, so there may be operational reasons for changes to applications, but we're yet to see an installation where applications are never ever touched after they are live.

The QlikView product itself doesn't stand still, and sometimes new features are worth implementing into existing applications. Always check out announcements about new features, and consider whether they would improve the applications already in your portfolio.

As well as new features in QlikView itself, your own skills will improve, and you will probably find better ways of doing things; so, it's always worth revisiting applications from time to time to check whether there are opportunities for improvement. We sometimes look at code that we wrote five years ago and ask ourselves, "Why did we do that? We could have used `<insert favorite new function>`, and it would have been so much better/more elegant/faster/impressive/all of these things!" We're also pretty sure that there are at least two ways of doing the same thing in QlikView, usually more like three or four. Which works best in your situation is for you to experiment with and find out.

Don't be afraid to experiment with QlikView. Take the time to skim through the list of functions from time to time and try out some that you've never used. Sometimes, they are just the thing you need in the next development. Making mistakes and breaking things are great ways to learn how to do things the right way – and this is true with QlikView as well. Remember that QlikView is one of those tools that fight back if you're doing things the wrong way. So, if you just can't get something to work the way you think it should, you're doing it wrong. Try a different approach but don't give up. We haven't found anything yet that can't be achieved in some way with QlikView.

Summary

In this chapter, we covered the very important topic of security with a detailed explanation of Section Access. We also looked at the deployment of a completed document and gave guidance on how to solve common problems that occur after deployment and how to look for ways to improve performance. We hope that you have found this book useful and enjoyable. *Happy Qlikking*!

Hidden Image List

The following is a list of over 450 graphical images and icons used within QlikView that you can add to your document with no overhead, load time, or distribution issues as they are part and parcel of QlikView Desktop and Server.

To use any of the graphics, you need to prefix the image name with this:

```
qmem://<bundled>/Images/
```

Then, set **Representation** to **Image**, as shown in the following screenshot:

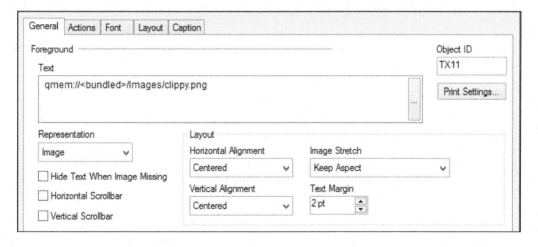

Hidden Image List

6_progress_bar_1.png	
6_progress_bar_2.png	
6_progress_bar_3.png	
6_progress_bar_4.png	
6_progress_bar_5.png	
6_progress_bar_6.png	
add.png	
add16x16.png	
annotation_notecount_bg.png	
annotation_notecount_selected_bg.png	
annotations-sprite.png	
aquaball.png	
aquatile.png	
aquatile2.png	
arrowdirectionboth.png	
arrowdirectionfilledboth.png	
arrowdirectionfilledleft.png	
arrowdirectionfilledright.png	
arrowdirectionleft.png	
arrowdirectionnone.png	
arrowdirectionright.png	
arrowmodeend.png	
arrowmodefilledend.png	
arrowmodefilledmiddle.png	
arrowmodemiddle.png	
bar_chart_1.png	
bar_chart_2.png	
bar_chart_3.png	
bar_chart_4.png	
bookmark.png	
bookmark_additive.png	
bookmark_layout.png	
bookmark_layout_additive.png	
brushedmetaltile.png	
calcdim.png	
calendar.png	
caption_menu.png	
checkbox_andselect_excluded.png	
checkbox_checked.png	
checkbox_checked_excluded.png	
checkbox_deselected.png	
checkbox_disabled.png	
checkbox_locked.png	
checkbox_locked_excluded.png	
checkbox_option.png	
checkindicator.png	
chevrondown.png	
chevronup.png	
clearothers.png	
clippy.png	
closemultibox.png	

colorexp.png	
copy.png	
copyimage.png	
cross.png	
cyclic.png	
delete.png	
delete16x16.png	
disabled_cross.png	
drilldown.png	
drillup.png	
emf_clear.emf	
emf_clear.png	
emf_excel.emf	
emf_excel.png	
emf_info.emf	
emf_info.png	
emf_lock.emf	
emf_lock.png	
emf_maximize.emf	
emf_maximize.png	
emf_minimize.emf	
emf_minimize.png	
emf_print.emf	
emf_print.png	
emf_questionmark.emf	
emf_questionmark.png	
emf_restore.emf	
emf_restore.png	
emf_search.emf	
emf_search.png	
emf_unlock.emf	
emf_unlock.png	
errorbar.png	
errorbar_hi.png	
errorbar_low.png	
expand.png	
expand_left.png	
expand_right.png	
fancy_error.png	
fancy_info.png	
fancy_question_mark.png	
fancy_warning.png	
fasttype_bar.png	
fasttype_block.png	
fasttype_combo.png	
fasttype_funnel.png	
fasttype_gauge.png	
fasttype_grid.png	
fasttype_line.png	
fasttype_mekko.png	
fasttype_pie.png	

Hidden Image List

fasttype_pivot.png	
fasttype_radar.png	
fasttype_scatter.png	
fasttype_straight.png	
fx.png	f(x)
gauge_chart_4.png	
headerfootertools16px.png	
hourglass.png	
icon_avatar_disabled_24.png	
icon_avatar_normal_24.png	
icon_back_disabled_24.png	
icon_back_normal_24.png	
icon_barchart.png	
icon_baroffset.png	
icon_blockchart.png	
icon_boxplot.png	
icon_clear.png	
icon_compactlist_down_24.png	
icon_compactlist_normal_24.png	
icon_delete_disabled_24.png	
icon_delete_normal_24.png	
icon_delete2_disabled_16.png	
icon_delete2_enabled_16.png	
icon_detailedlist_down_24.png	
icon_detailedlist_normal_24.png	
icon_edit_disabled_24.png	
icon_edit_normal_24.png	
icon_gaugechart.png	
icon_group_disabled_24.png	
icon_group_normal_24.png	
icon_image.png	
icon_linechart.png	
icon_linestyle.png	
icon_lock.png	
icon_note_disabled_24.png	
icon_note_normal_24.png	
icon_piechart.png	
icon_piepopout.png	
icon_popup.png	
icon_scatterchart.png	
icon_scrolldown_disabled_14.png	
icon_scrolldown_normal_14.png	
icon_scrollup_disabled_14.png	
icon_scrollup_normal_14.png	
icon_setting_disabled_24.png	
icon_setting_normal_24.png	
icon_showvalue.png	
icon_snapshot_disabled_24.png	
icon_snapshot_normal_24.png	
icon_snapshot_selected_24.png	
icon_stockplot.png	

Appendix

minichartmode_bar.png	
minichartmode_dots.png	
minichartmode_line.png	
minichartmode_line_dots.png	
minichartmode_whisker.png	
note_bg_off.png	
note_bg_on.png	
object_refresh.png	
object_stop.png	
openmultibox.png	
pausebutton.png	
pie_chart_1.png	
pie_chart_2.png	
pie_chart_4.png	
pivot_chart_1.png	
pivot_chart_2.png	
pivot_chart_3.png	
pivot_chart_4.png	
pivot_collapse.png	
pivot_expand.png	
playbutton.png	
preview_no_border.png	
preview_raised_border.png	
preview_sunken_border.png	
preview_thin_border.png	
preview_walled_border.png	
print_orientation_landscape.png	
print_orientation_portrait.png	
programicon32x32.png	
programicon48x48.png	
progress_bar_1of5.png	
progress_bar_2of5.png	
progress_bar_3of5.png	
progress_bar_4of5.png	
progress_bar_5of5.png	
progress_bar_intro.png	
radio_checked.png	
radio_checked_excluded.png	
radio_option.png	
radio_option_excluded.png	
refresh.png	
report.png	
reportdlgitemsettings.png	
reportdlgnewimage.png	
reportdlgnewselstamp.png	
reportdlgnewtext.png	
reportdlgpagesettings.png	
reportdlgreportsettings.png	
scriptwiz_edit_16x16.png	
scriptwiz_edit_dark_16x16.png	
selectall.png	

```
selectexcluded.png
selectpossible.png
settings16x16.png
shared.png
singlepaper.png
splash.png
spreadsheetmaxicon.bmp
spreadsheetminicon.bmp
spreadsheettagbcd.bmp
spreadsheettagint.bmp
spreadsheettagreal.bmp
spreadsheettagtext.bmp
spreadsheettaguint.bmp
startdialogtop.png
startpageexample.png
startpagefavfileicon.png
startpagefavfileothericon.png
startpagefavfileotherremoteicon.png
startpagefavremotefileicon.png
startpagefileicon.png
startpagefileiconsmall.png
startpagefileothericon.png
startpagefileotherremoteicon.png
startpagefoldericon.png
startpagegettingstarted.png
startpagego.png
startpagelicenseinfo.png
startpageopenedfoldericon.png
startpageremotefileicon.png
startpageserver.png
startpagetopbackground.png
startpagetopleft.png
startpagetoptile.png
style_2d3dpie.bmp
style_2dpie.bmp
style_2dpie_bevel.bmp
style_2dpie_bowl.bmp
style_2dpie_normal3ddonut.bmp
style_2dpie_normaldonut.bmp
style_2dpie_thick3ddonut.bmp
style_2dpie_thickdonut.bmp
style_2dpie_thin3ddonut.bmp
style_2dpie_thindonut.bmp
style_3dpie.bmp
style_bar_grouped.bmp
style_bar_horizontal.bmp
style_bar_stacked.bmp
style_bar_vert_2d.bmp
style_bar_vert_3d.bmp
style_bar_vert_3dtube.bmp
style_bar_vert_block.bmp
```

Hidden Image List

- style_bar_vert_plastic.bmp
- style_bar_vert_shadow.bmp
- style_bar_vert_tube.bmp
- style_bar_vertical.bmp
- style_block.bmp
- style_block_caption.bmp
- style_combo_2d.bmp
- style_combo_plastic.bmp
- style_combo_shadow.bmp
- style_funnel_plain1.bmp
- style_gauge_circular.bmp
- style_gauge_leddisplay.bmp
- style_gauge_reflectedtube.bmp
- style_gauge_speedometer.bmp
- style_gauge_straight.bmp
- style_gauge_testtube.bmp
- style_gauge_trafficlight.bmp
- style_grid_3dball.bmp
- style_grid_ball.bmp
- style_grid_circle.bmp
- style_grid_pie.bmp
- style_grid_single_ball.bmp
- style_grid_single_circle.bmp
- style_grid_single_cross.bmp
- style_grid_single_plus.bmp
- style_grid_unisize_pie.bmp
- style_line_3d.bmp
- style_line_3darea.bmp
- style_line_and_symbols.bmp
- style_line_area.bmp
- style_line_plain.bmp
- style_line_shadow.bmp
- style_line_symbolsonly.bmp
- style_mekko.bmp
- style_mekko_normalized.bmp
- style_pivot.bmp
- style_pivot_all_left.bmp
- style_pivot_crosstable.bmp
- style_radar_area.bmp
- style_radar_standard.bmp
- style_scatter_bubble_3dball.bmp
- style_scatter_bubble_ball.bmp
- style_scatter_bubble_circle.bmp
- style_scatter_multi.bmp
- style_scatter_single_ball.bmp
- style_scatter_single_circle.bmp
- style_scatter_single_cross.bmp
- style_scatter_single_plus.bmp
- style_straight.bmp
- style_true3dpie.bmp
- table_chart_1.png

Appendix

table_chart_2.png	
table_chart_3.png	
table_chart_4.png	
tablegroup.png	
textcolorexp.png	
textfmtexp.png	
toolicons.png	
toolicons32.png	
webicon_accessadd.png	
webicon_axis.png	
webicon_barchart.png	
webicon_bkgcolor.png	
webicon_blockchart.png	
webicon_bookmarkobject.png	
webicon_button.png	
webicon_calendar.png	
webicon_calendar_img.png	
webicon_clearactive.png	
webicon_clearother.png	
webicon_clone.png	
webicon_close.png	
webicon_color.png	
webicon_combochart.png	
webicon_container.png	
webicon_create.png	
webicon_currentselections.png	
webicon_dbg.png	
webicon_design_off.png	
webicon_design_on.png	
webicon_down.png	
webicon_dropinsert.png	
webicon_excel.png	
webicon_expredit.png	
webicon_fastchange.png	
webicon_filter.png	
webicon_fittoimage.png	
webicon_font.png	
webicon_funnelchart.png	
webicon_gaugechart.png	
webicon_gridchart.png	
webicon_help.png	
webicon_helpicon.png	
webicon_hide.png	
webicon_image.png	
webicon_inputbox.png	
webicon_iso.png	
webicon_linearrow.png	
webicon_linechart.png	
webicon_listbox.png	
webicon_lockselection.png	
webicon_maximize.png	

Hidden Image List

Index

A

applications
  deploying, on to production 149
  deploying, to UAT 149
  improving 156, 157
architecture, QlikView
  about 5
  background 5
  implementation 6-9
Autonumber() function
  using 112

B

backups
  creating 41, 42

C

calculations
  performing 103-107
calendars
  adding 89-91
change management
  considerations 28-30
charts
  chart expressions, reusing 121
  customizing 122-124
Circular Reference 56
coding tips
  about 97
  constant coding style, using 98
  MUST_INCLUDE, using 98
  stringing, with script 98
  version numbers, mentioning 98

D

data
  dealing with 54
  maintaining, in different documents 65, 66
data model
  design, simplifying 85-89
  loops, avoiding 83, 84
  subtables, avoiding 85-89
Data Quality
  duplicate entries, removing 65
  handling 61, 62
  inconsistent data, handling 63, 64
  incorrect or erroneous data, handling 62
data sources
  obtaining, from web page 99, 100
date selection
  adding 89-91
developer environment
  best practices 47, 48
  max values, in current selections 41
  most recently used files, viewing 40
  search settings 40
  selection appearance 40
  setting up 38, 39
document names
  creating 26-28
document recovery
  performing 41, 42

E

Easter eggs
  about 48
  implementing 49-51

Enterprise Edition
  versus Small Business Edition 31, 32
environments, QlikView
  about 5
  background 5
  Development 6
  implementation 6-9
  multiple machines 7
  Production 6
  single machine 6
  Test 6
  three machines 7
  two machines 6
expressions
  caching 116
  copying 120

F

flags, script 103-107

G

global settings
  Always Show Design Menu Items 46, 47
  Always Use Logfiles for New
      Documents 46
  Default Styling Mode, using 44, 45
  implementing 43
golden source
  about 151
  implementing 151, 152

H

Help Text
  using 124-127
hidden graphics
  adding 122

I

include files
  using 101
incremental load
  about 71
  implementing 71-74

infrastructure, QlikView
  background 1
  implementation 2-4
  need for 1

J

JOIN function
  problems, avoiding 92-95

L

license types
  about 35
  implementing 36-38
  Leased License (Named User) 35
  Personal Edition 35
  Stand Alone (Local Client) 35
list box
  creating 56-59
logs
  modifying 102
Loop and Reduce 32

M

maintainable environment
  background 9
  building 9
  implementation 10-12
maximum date
  searching 110, 111
Memory Statistics
  about 153
  using 153-156
minimum date
  searching 110, 111
multiple selection criteria
  handling 117-119

O

objects
  resizing 127, 128
  stopping 128-130
optimal server settings
  reference link 5
Optimized Load 67

P

Peek() function
  using 108
performance optimization
  considering 71-75
preceding loads
  about 109
  using 109, 110
Previous() function
  using 108
prototype
  creating 60, 61
  reference link 60
Publisher
  about 32
  drawbacks 152, 153
  features 33
  Section Access, using 146

Q

QlikView
  do's and don'ts 51, 52
QlikView Directory Service Connector (DSC) 7
QlikView Distribution Service 7
QlikView Management Service (QMS) 7
QlikView projects
  about 12
  background 13
  considerations 14
  data model, developing 15
  implementation 13, 14
  project proposal, reviewing 14
QlikView server
  Enterprise Edition 31
  Small Business Edition 31
QlikView Server (QVS) 7
QlikView Web Server (QVWS) 7
QVD layers
  structure, building 67-70

R

reusable environment
  background 9
  building 9
  implementation 10-12

S

screen performance
  optimizing 115, 116
script
  calculations, performing 103-107
  flags 103-107
scroll bar
  defaulting 131-133
Section Access
  used, for security 138-143
  with Data Reduction 146
  with Publisher 146
security
  adding 135
  additional parameters, adding 144, 145
  considerations 28-30
  Document CALs 136
  fields, hiding 143
  Physical Network Access 136
  Section Access, using 138-143
  with Publisher 136, 137
server jobs failures
  antivirus software, using 149
  connection failures 147
  Excel spreadsheets, using 147
  QlikView engines, using 148
  QVD file, overwriting 149
  reasons 147
  relative path, using 148
set analysis
  adding 89-91
site standards
  creating 17-22
  enforcing 17-22
site-style template
  designing 22-26

Small Business Edition
  versus Enterprise Edition 31, 32
spreadsheet
  reading 112, 113
synthetic keys
  creating 77-80

T

table box
  creating 56-59
tables
  linking 80-83
Task Management 33
timeboxing 13

U

UAT
  applications, deploying 150
User Licenses (CALs)
  about 31
  Document 34
  Named User 34
  Session 34
  Usage 34

W

Windows Task Manager
  about 153
  using 153-156

Thank you for buying
Qlikview Unlocked

About Packt Publishing

Packt, pronounced 'packed', published its first book, *Mastering phpMyAdmin for Effective MySQL Management*, in April 2004, and subsequently continued to specialize in publishing highly focused books on specific technologies and solutions.

Our books and publications share the experiences of your fellow IT professionals in adapting and customizing today's systems, applications, and frameworks. Our solution-based books give you the knowledge and power to customize the software and technologies you're using to get the job done. Packt books are more specific and less general than the IT books you have seen in the past. Our unique business model allows us to bring you more focused information, giving you more of what you need to know, and less of what you don't.

Packt is a modern yet unique publishing company that focuses on producing quality, cutting-edge books for communities of developers, administrators, and newbies alike. For more information, please visit our website at www.packtpub.com.

About Packt Enterprise

In 2010, Packt launched two new brands, Packt Enterprise and Packt Open Source, in order to continue its focus on specialization. This book is part of the Packt Enterprise brand, home to books published on enterprise software – software created by major vendors, including (but not limited to) IBM, Microsoft, and Oracle, often for use in other corporations. Its titles will offer information relevant to a range of users of this software, including administrators, developers, architects, and end users.

Writing for Packt

We welcome all inquiries from people who are interested in authoring. Book proposals should be sent to author@packtpub.com. If your book idea is still at an early stage and you would like to discuss it first before writing a formal book proposal, then please contact us; one of our commissioning editors will get in touch with you.

We're not just looking for published authors; if you have strong technical skills but no writing experience, our experienced editors can help you develop a writing career, or simply get some additional reward for your expertise.

QlikView for Developers Cookbook

ISBN: 978-1-78217-973-3 Paperback: 290 pages

Discover the strategies needed to tackle the most challenging tasks facing the QlikView developer

1. Learn beyond QlikView training.
2. Discover QlikView Advanced GUI development, advanced scripting, complex data modelling issues, and much more.
3. Accelerate the growth of your QlikView developer ability.
4. Based on over 7 years' experience of QlikView development.

QlikView 11 for Developers

ISBN: 978-1-84968-606-8 Paperback: 534 pages

Develop Business Intelligence applications with QlikView 11

1. Learn to build applications for Business Intelligence while following a practical case -- HighCloud Airlines. Each chapter develops parts of the application and it evolves throughout the book along with your own QlikView skills.
2. The code bundle for each chapter can be accessed on your local machine without having to purchase a QlikView license.
3. The hands-on approach allows you to build a QlikView application that integrates real data from several different sources and presents it in dashboards, analyses and reports.

Please check **www.PacktPub.com** for information on our titles

Learning Qlik Sense
The Official Guide

ISBN: 978-1-78217-335-9   Paperback: 230 pages

Get to grips with the vision of Qlik Sense for next generation business intelligence and data discovery

1. Get insider insight on Qlik Sense and its new approach to business intelligence.
2. Create your own Qlik Sense applications, and administer server architecture.
3. Explore practical demonstrations for utilizing Qlik Sense to discover data for sales, human resources, and more.

Learning QlikView Data Visualization

ISBN: 978-1-78217-989-4   Paperback: 156 pages

Visualize and analyze data with the most intuitive business intelligence tool, QlikView

1. Explore the basics of data discovery with QlikView.
2. Perform rank, trend, multivariate, distribution, correlation, geographical, and what-if analysis.
3. Deploy data visualization best practices for bar, line, scatterplot, heat map, tables, histogram, box plot, and geographical charts.

Please check **www.PacktPub.com** for information on our titles

Lightning Source UK Ltd.
Milton Keynes UK
UKOW04f1101161016

285381UK00001B/33/P